RUGBY *FOR*
THREE-QUARTERS

with Richard Hill

RUGBY FOR THREE-QUARTERS

with Richard Hill

Peter Johnson

A & C Black · London

First published 1993 by
A & C Black (Publishers) Ltd
35 Bedford Row, London WC1R 4JH

© 1993 Peter Johnson & Richard Hill

ISBN 0 7136 3782 X

A CIP catalogue record for this book
is available from the British Library.

Acknowledgements
Photographs on pages 30–1, 35, 37, 39 and 59 courtesy of Bristol United Press. All other photographs courtesy of Allsport UK Ltd.

Design and illustrations by Eric Drewery.

Typeset by Wyvern Typesetting, Bristol, Avon.
Printed and bound in Great Britain by The Bath Press, Avon.

CONTENTS

FOREWORD

There is no doubt that at both club and national level English rugby has experienced a remarkable transformation over the last four years. The onset of the new leagues has focused coaches, players and administrators alike on improving performance. Standards of fitness have advanced (although still, in my opinion, not yet to satisfactory levels), players are working harder at their individual skills, and the new crop of mini rugby talent is now entering the senior game. English rugby is looking good. But before favourable comparisons can be drawn with the game in Australia and New Zealand, we need to raise coaching standards so as to impart the knowledge gained at international level to the lower echelons of the sport.

I enrolled on the RFU Intermediate Coaching Award scheme because I felt strongly that both youngsters and senior players needed better coaching. One of the organisers of the course was Peter Johnson, an extremely experienced coach who has been involved for many years in rugby coaching at Colston's Collegiate School and Bristol RFC, and with the South West division.

Peter has studied three-quarter play in great depth: this book is the result of this thorough analysis. He understands that three-quarter play is now very complex, and that more thought and planning has to be devoted to club training nights. It is clear from my involvement at Bath RFC and as a member of the England squad, that it is becoming increasingly more difficult to score tries. Sides are becoming much better organised in defence. The same old moves are no longer sufficient. Opponents will simply anticipate and counteract these moves if they have been seen many times before. The modern game is desperate for new and varied three-quarter moves, for new ideas to surprise the opposition.

There is not always the time during a match to complicate proceedings. The simple manoeuvres, performed at pace, will often be more successful than a convoluted ploy. But how can the basics be taught week after week without training becoming boring? This book will provide the coach and the player with many different ideas and lesson plans to be used in the progression to develop the required skills. Use the drills to inject fresh enthusiasm into training sessions, and to begin to get players to think hard about how they can break down defensive formations. Give them the exercises, let them solve the puzzle. Then leave them to make their own split-second decisions.

Rugby for Three-quarters provides a comprehensive guide to the technical and tactical demands of successful three-quarter play. I wholeheartedly endorse the theory and drills it contains, drills that have been tried and tested at the very highest level.

Richard Hill

INTRODUCTION

This book has been written for coaches, captains and three-quarters with the aim of generating greater insights into rugby union three-quarter play.

Part I is the theory, the explanation of the basic principles, positional requirements, options, organisation of three-quarter lines and key factors in individual skills. Parts II and III are for coaches to refer to when stuck for ideas on training nights. Here they will find exercises for individuals, positions and units. After the warm-up, choose an exercise or two from Part II as an introduction to the unit exercise from Part III.

There is no one way to align the three-quarter line. The critical factors are space, time and the intentions of the fly-half. Other considerations are the speed and the quality of the delivery of the ball. What happens during the second phase is fundamentally the decision of an individual, and whether space, time and numbers are to his advantage.

Generally, all that three-quarters seem to want to do in training are moves. There should be less emphasis on moves and more on individual skills. Moves are important from set pieces to disrupt the defensive patterns of the opposition. But rarely do moves result in tries, except in an attacking position inside the opposition 22-metre area. The principles of moves or ploys are explained. If these are grasped, then a line can perform any move they can invent. Actual ploys have not been included here.

Note Throughout the book rugby players and coaches are referred to individually as 'he'. This should, of course, be taken to mean 'he or she' where appropriate.

Definitions

The reader may find the following definitions useful.

Alignment: the formation of the three-quarters when starting their attack or defence. The alignment of three-quarters can be steep or flat, i.e. at a very deep or a very narrow angle to the scrum, ruck, maul or line-out.

Gain line: an imaginary line running across the pitch at right angles to the touch line. It runs through the middle of the line-out, scrum, ruck and maul. If a player with the ball crosses it, then he is making ground and all players in his team are going forwards.

Passing line: an imaginary line along which the ball travels. If the attacking three-quarter line makes passes too far from the tackle line, i.e. too far from the opposition, then the defenders will not be 'fixed' and they will be able to drift out on to the out-side attackers. Then these outside attackers, e.g. the wingers and the full-back, will be confronted by several defenders.

Ploys: planned and rehearsed tactical moves for different positions in the field and from the different types of first phase possession. If opposing three-quarter lines have not been disrupted by a back row move, a three-quarter move can be employed from second phase possession.

Running line: the angle at which players run in attack or defence in relation to the goal line. If a player is on a straight running line, he is keeping his hips and shoulders square and parallel with the goal line. If he is running on a diagonal, he is running with his hips and shoulders pointing at the touch line at a variety of angles to the goal line. If he is running on an arc, he is first running on a diagonal, but straightening up before he gets the ball so that he is running towards the goal line.

Spacing: the distance between each three-quarter when lined up. If wide apart, passing becomes more difficult to execute and space on the outside is used up.

Tackle line: the imaginary line where the defending and attacking three-quarter lines meet. Assuming that both three-quarter lines are travelling at the same speed, then the tackle line is exactly half-way between their starting positions. This usually means that the tackle line is rarely reached by an attacking three-quarter line because players are tackled before they reach it.

PART I

THEORY

GENERAL PRINCIPLES OF THREE-QUARTER PLAY

● Have at your disposal a selection of moves. Be flexible, and be sure of what you are trying to achieve.

● Commit the opposition. Run straight at the opposing three-quarters and 'involve' them. Do not run across the pitch and thereby reduce the space on the outside.

● Play the numbers game. Seven three-quarters play like ten by passing, running and getting involved again in the movement. Subtract defenders and add attackers.

● Absorb pressure. Consider the distance to the gain line because it affects the tackle line. Consider the time allowed by the opposition and what obstacles there might be before the gain line.

● Keep possession of the ball. Try to stay on your feet when tackled and make the ball available to your support. Do not kick the ball away aimlessly. Kick only to recover possession.

● There must be immediate support of the ball carrier. When a break has been achieved, the whole line must surge through. Support kicks ahead. There must be designated chasers.

● Position: run straight to preserve the space outside, check the cross cover, make it difficult for the tackler, and make it easier to support from the inside. Come from depth to take a flat pass, thus giving the cover defence less time – and the flatter the pass, the straighter the run. Put the ball into space. Give the attack width to make it harder for the defender to catch the receiver, and force the cross cover to go further.

● Tackle effectively. Defence can be turned into attack by good tackles. It is possible to be going forwards even when not in possession of the ball by pressurising the opposition. Be organised in defence.

● Cover: in defence get between the ball and your own goal line. If the ball has been kicked behind you, the three-quarters should turn quickly and get back faster than if they were in support of a break. Any move should have a fail safe, e.g. the blind-side winger covers the full-back who has joined the line.

● Speed is essential – speed of pass, of thought, and over the ground. Take off quickly, run with control, bring the defence on to you. A change of pace or angle of running can be added somewhere in the line to get the opposition to do something to your advantage, or to disrupt their defence patterns. If everything is done at pace there is less time to cover and there is a greater likelihood of driving through tackles.

Key words

POSSESSION   POSITION   PACE
SUPPORT   PRESSURE   COVER

POSITIONAL REQUIREMENTS

Scrum-half

● Priorities:
(i)   pass quickly and accurately to the fly-half
(ii) run in attack
(iii) kick in attack and defence
(iv) defend against back-row moves.

● The ideal scrum-half is left-handed and right-footed because:
(i)   he would use the left hand when passing from scrums since he follows the path of the ball through the scrum from left to right, and so it is more natural to pass off the left hand to the right
(ii) this also means that his body is between the ball and the opposing scrum-half, thus providing protection for the pass
(iii) scrums on the right side of the field often demand pivot passes off the left hand, again to provide that protection
(iv) however, because peripheral vision is lost, some might prefer to move to the right-hand side of the no. 8 and pass off the right hand. Then there may be a chance of an interception by the opposing scrum-half, unless the fly-half stands deep. A possible solution is for the no. 8 to pick up and feed the scrum-half so he can use his right hand, but this inevitably slows proceedings.

(v) line-outs on the left side of the field also involve the use of the left-handed pass. The pivot pass, where the scrum-half swivels on his heels and falls away from the opposition, is dangerous. It is possible to intercept such a pass. Also, the scrum-half loses peripheral vision and may not see the opposition's open-side flanker flying at the fly-half. The dive pass would be better here

(vi) generally, the only position where a right-handed pass would be made from set piece play is from a line-out on the right side of the field

(vii) from loose play, the scrum-half generally has a greater choice. Much depends on which side of the ruck or maul the fly-half wants to go.

🖚 The most important ingredients for a good scrum-half pass are **speed** and **accuracy**. **Length of pass** does help the fly-half avoid pressure from the back row, but at the expense of space wide out.

🖚 The **dive pass** is generally used in wet conditions or when the ball shoots back awkwardly behind the scrum-half. Often it is used when the scrum-half is weak in passing off his left hand.

🖚 The **standing pass** allows the scrum-half to support immediately. The dive pass temporarily puts the scrum-half out of the game.

🖚 The scrum-half stands at the front of the line-out and follows the ball in because:
(i) his jumpers can see him all the time
(ii) he has full vision of the field
(iii) he is giving no indication to the opposition about where the ball might be thrown.

Fly-half

🖚 Priorities:
(i) pass the ball and launch an attack
(ii) kick in attack and defence
(iii) in defence, bring up his centres on to the opposition's midfield.

🖚 Should the fly-half take the ball standing still or running on to it?
(i) If he runs on to the pass, he closes the distance between his own line and the defending line, thus putting pressure on his own centres.
(ii) If he receives the ball standing still, the back row and his

opposite number lose interest in him and can drift on to the centres. A drift defence is easy to employ. If he is used as a pivot, the inside centre becomes the decision-maker.

(iii) Some sort of movement is necessary to 'interest' the defenders, but not so much as to make life difficult for the centres.

(iv) Move when the ball is in the scrum-half's hands or when it is in the air, but do not creep forwards before then.

(v) From second phase he can take the ball at pace. The further along the line he wants to strike, however, governs how deep he takes the ball.

🏉 At what angle should the fly-half run?

(i) If at right angles to the line of pass, it is easier to receive the scrum-half pass. But then:
 – he has to give the fall away pass to help straighten the line and interest the defence
 – the inside centre must be responsible for straightening the line by standing wide and running in a straight line.

(ii) If on a straight run, then he will interest the opposition and hold them close in.

How deep should the fly-half stand?

(i) If he lies deep and runs straight, the converging open-side flanker has to change his angle of run to get amongst the midfield.

(ii) If he is shallow and wide, he pulls the open-side flanker on to his centres.

(iii) If he is shallow and close, he interests the open-side flanker and the fly-half, and he keeps the space wide out.

(iv) The length of pass of the scrum-half, and where the ball is thrown, determines where the fly-half stands at line-outs.
 – If he stands near the end of the line-out, he can interest the back row and be shielded by his own back row.
 – If he stands wide, he can be beyond the reach of the back row and commit the opposing fly-half.
 – He can sometimes take a flat ball to attack the tail of the line-out, get across the gain line quickly, and hit at the weak point of a drift defence.

Centres

🏉 Should the centres play inside and outside, or left and right?

(i) The inside centre must be able to pass quickly and kick as well as a fly-half. He must also be able to tackle well.

(ii)   The outside centre needs to be a good attacking player.

(iii)   A left centre has to defend more often because of the way the ball is used by the opposition from scrums.

(iv)   A right centre needs to be a more attacking player because he sees more of the ball.

⬤   The centres should vary the length of their passes and their spacing between each other – play 'concertina'. This sometimes allows the centres to take the ball in gaps.

⬤   If the fly-half misses out the inside centre and passes directly to the outside centre, then he becomes the play-maker. It opens up a lot of attacking possibilities as he can pass to a number of players – the open-side winger, the full-back, the inside centre or the blind-side winger.

Wingers

⬤   Left winger:

(i)   if left-footed, he can keep the ball in play by kicking ahead

(ii)   if right-footed, he can be used in defence to kick the ball to touch

(iii)   he needs to be proficient defensively because most attacks will be launched at him.

⬤   Right winger: the more attacking player because he gets the ball more often (even though off left-handed passes) because of the play off scrums.

Full-back

⬤   Priorities:

(i)   to be safe under the high ball

(ii)   to kick accurately

(iii)   to enter the three-quarter line decisively

(iv)   to counter-attack effectively

(v)   to tackle as a last line of defence.

⬤   The full-back should never get caught with the ball behind his own forwards. He has several options when fielding a ball:

(i)   he can make a mark within the limits of the existing laws

(ii)   he can kick to touch to give time for his forwards to re-group

(iii)   he can counter-attack, if time and space are available, by:

– employing a high kick so that his forwards have time to get back between the ball and their own goal line. He will

also have the chance of regaining possession by chasing the ball
- running and linking with his wingers (*see* pages 27–9).

The ability to enter the three-quarter line in attack is very important. The further away from his own goal line, the further out he comes into the line. On his own goal line, his defensive and kicking abilities are useful and he should be standing close to the fly-half. Inside the opposition's 22-metre area, the full-back should be coming into the line outside the winger.

If the midfield is doing its job properly, and the defence is well organised with the blind-side winger acting as a sweeper, the full-back's least important role is as a tackler. Attacks should be snuffed out before they ever reach the full-back.

Scrum-half break: start low; use short strides; carry the ball in two hands ready to pass to the support; keep the head up and scan the field in front

OPTIONS IN ATTACK

🏉 Outflank the defence. This is not easy to do from first phase possession and it may be necessary to disrupt the defence by creating second phase play and then attacking the disorganised opposition.

🏉 Break through the defence. This is usually achieved by set moves and sometimes by a player's individual elusive skills.

🏉 Go over a defence.
(i) A high kick and chase into the box or towards the posts gives a 50% chance of recovering possession.
(ii) A chip kick over a rapidly advancing midfield.
(iii) A long diagonal kick for the open-side winger to chase.

🏉 Counter-attack from a poor opposition kick.

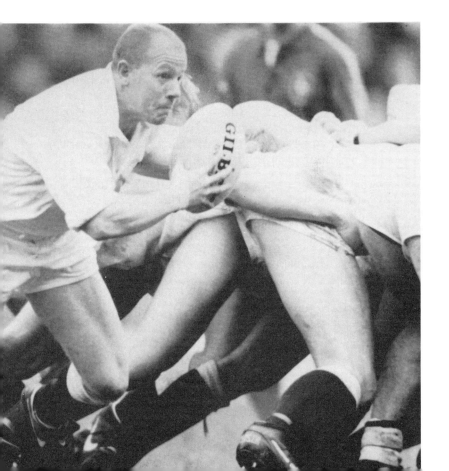

Possession from scrums

⬤ Possession from scrums is generally assured and should be used positively.

⬤ The midfield is always under pressure.

(i) The attack should hold the defenders in midfield with decoy moves, and pass the ball to players with more time and space on the edge of the midfield.

(ii) Cut-out passes, which avoid passing the ball through too many pairs of hands, also relieve the pressure, and the ball can be moved wider more quickly.

⬤ Options from a scrum on the left side of the field.

(i) Move the ball wide because:
  – it tends to be a quicker pass from the scrum-half
  – the open-side flanker's first priority here is to watch for someone breaking close to the scrum, and so the fly-half is his second priority. This gives the fly-half a little more time
  – the scrum-half pass to the fly-half tends to be flatter, so the fly-half can run straighter and the midfield can be on a shallow alignment.

(ii) Kick into the box, towards the posts, chip over the midfield or 'kick the diagonal' (across the pitch from left to right) because the fly-half has his right leg protected, being further away from potential tacklers.

(iii) The fly-half can pass to the full-back going down the narrow side. The long pass will be off the fly-half's right hand.

⬤ Options from a scrum on the right side of the field.

(i) Play the ball wide? This is very difficult because:
  – the scrum-half's pass is slower and more difficult, tending to be a pivot pass
  – the fly-half has to stand deeper because of the chances of the opposing scrum-half intercepting the pass, and also so that the scrum-half can see him as he is making a pivot pass
  – the open-side flanker does not have to worry so much about a scrum-half break and his first priority is the fly-half, so he can concentrate on getting to him quickly
  – it is better, therefore, for the fly-half to take the ball standing still and for the centres to delay their run.

(ii) Attack the narrow side with varying combinations of the back row, scrum-half, right winger, full-back. It is possible to create overlaps here because the opposing scrum-half is left on the far side of the scrum, and an attack to the right should have the advantage of numbers.

(iii) Switches are better because:
  - the fly-half tends to be deep to receive a pivot pass. He tends to run across as a result
  - the open-side flanker can over-commit himself to catching the fly-half.

● Options from a midfield scrum.

(i)   Use the fly-half as a decoy or pivot.
  - He tends to stand behind the scrum and so he must run across.
  - Perhaps use a centre or the full-back to receive the pass from the scrum-half.

(ii) The defence is split and stretched. There are many moves which can be employed to create overlaps.

Possession from line-outs

● Possession from line-outs can be better for the three-quarters than scrum ball, provided it is delivered quickly, e.g. off the top of the jump straight into the scrum-half's hands, because:

(i)   there is greater width to the attack
(ii) the defending three-quarters are further away
(iii) scrum-half passes can be easier and flatter.

● Where the ball is thrown in the line-out is very important to the three-quarters because of the length of the scrum-half pass.

(i)   If thrown to no. 2 jumper, the opposing open-side flanker is close to the fly-half.

(ii) If thrown to the no. 4 jumper, the fly-half has a little more room by being further from the flanker. The ball is more secure thrown to here than to the tail of the line-out.

(iii) However, if the ball is thrown to the back of the line-out, it is the best type of ball for the three-quarters because the opposing back row is immediately engaged and sucked in.

● It can be argued that it is easier to defend from a line-out. The defenders have greater time to react to moves, and drift defences have cancelled out the extra man coming into the line from the full-back position or from the blind-side wing. However, drift defences can be dealt with. Better lines of running and more thought about how the ball is delivered from line-outs can solve most problems posed by the defence.

Possession from rucks and mauls

🏉 Mauls tend to give a team more options than rucks.
(i)   The scrum-half can control the delivery of the ball: his head is up and he can scan the field in front of him.
(ii) The forwards can roll off and commit any defenders who are standing off.

🏉 Possession for the three-quarters from **rucks**, however, tends to be better because:
(i)   it is more dynamic. Rucks give a quick delivery of the ball when the opposing three-quarters are still on their heels
(ii)   mauls tend to produce the ball slowly, thus giving the defence time to organise
(iii) it is easier for the fly-half and three-quarters to time their runs from rucks because they can see the ball all the time
(iv)   however, the delivery of the ball cannot be so well controlled from rucks, and the scrum-half cannot scan the field so well because his head is down as he is picking up the ball.

🏉 Where should the fly-half take the ball?
(i)   Sometimes, he should take a flat pass to cross the gain line as quickly as possible so the defence is still retreating.
(ii)   The further along the line that the fly-half wants to strike, the deeper he must take the ball so that the players outside him can get away their passes before being tackled.

OUTFLANKING A DEFENCE

🏉 **Time** and **space** are created for the winger by:
(i)   correct **alignment**
(ii)   **running lines** which commit the opposition's back row and midfield
(iii) **quick** and **accurate passes**.

🏉 **Width**, i.e. spacing, in the three-quarters can also help the winger outflank the defence, but:
(i)   having to give a long pass often cuts down the speed of its execution
(ii)   space is reduced for the winger
(iii) passes have to be very accurate. Players standing close together should catch a pass that is slightly bad, e.g. a little high. However, the further away from each other that the players stand, the more the differential increases. The slightly bad pass it not going to be caught because it will go over the receiver's head!

Alignment

⬤ The traditional alignment.

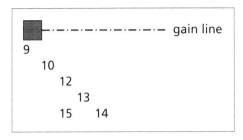

KEY	◼ scrum	● cone
	- - - - → pass	x attacker
	↑ running line	○ defender
	▬▬▬ line-out	◖ ball
	◼◼ tackle shield	▲ tackle bag

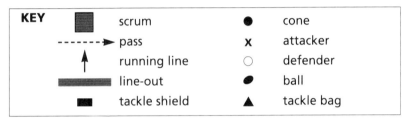

The line stands deep and wide from all types of possession.
(i)   The advantages are that:
– it relieves the immediate pressure and each three-quarter can get away his pass
– players can run at top speed.
(ii) The disadvantages are that:
– the forwards have a long way back to run to cover any mistakes which might occur
– the tackle line is a long way behind the forwards and the gain line
– the cover defence has time to get across the field
– it is easier to organise a drift defence
– if the fly-half takes a late decision to kick, then the three-quarters are too far behind to chase
– the three-quarters have to run long distances.

⬤ Saucer alignment.

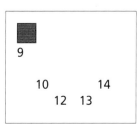

The fly-half acts as a pivot, takes the ball standing still and passes immediately. The centres stand shallow. Each three-quarter only runs when the ball is in the inside player's hands, so there is a steady acceleration along the line. The winger will have to stand level if not in front of the outside centre, otherwise he may get left behind. The pass is always flat and the three-quarters stand close together and run straight.

(i) The advantages are that:
  – it encourages straighter angles of running
  – it prevents a drift defence
  – the tackle line is closer to the forwards and to the gain line
  – all the three-quarters are running at pace
  – it keeps the space on the outside.

(ii) The disadvantages are that:
  – all the three-quarters have to be quick passers and be able to accept pressure from the defenders
  – although starting positions can be modified to cope with different abilities and skills, generally these three-quarters must be quick off the mark
  – the fly-half takes the ball standing still, which means the defence has little to worry about from him and so the back row can move on to the centres.

Australian schoolboys.

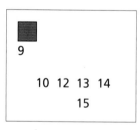

The fly-half lies fairly deep but all the three-quarters stand close and pass immediately. After passing, they each loop to the end.

(i) The advantages are that:
  – the winger has more space in which to operate
  – the winger gets the ball very early and receives immediate support
  – it spreads confusion in the defence, and looping players can attack gaps.

(ii) The disadvantages are:
  – very fast three-quarters are needed
  – they must have good peripheral vision.

Comments.

(i) Alignment depends on the individual skills and talents of each three-quarter. Each player should decide his own starting position so that he is running on to the pass, he can get his own pass away, and he is never too far from his forwards or the gain line. The passing line in relation to the tackle line is what is critical here. If close to the defenders, the attackers cannot drift; if too far from them, the defenders can move on to the outside players.

(ii) Consider variations of alignment from different types of possession, and to avoid predictability.

(iii) The inside centre should take into account that many fly-halves run across. He might find himself taking a pass too close to the fly-half or running across to avoid bumping into him. He should start wide so that he can receive the pass running straight.

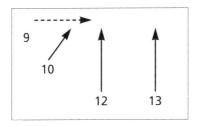

Running lines

There is a tendency for most three-quarters to start their running at an angle because:

(i) the fly-half does likewise, and it is easier for him to take the scrum-half's pass if he does so, but the other three-quarters generally take his lead

(ii) many three-quarters receive a pass as they are drifting away from the passer. This again makes it easier to catch and get the pass away

(iii) after the pass the passer tends to sink his hip and fall away. This straightens the line, but by then it is too late (*see* pages 51–8).

The reasons for straight running are:

(i) it makes it more difficult for the tackler because:
   – he is confronted with the head-on tackle
   – the ball carrier can side-step either side of him

(ii) by running across the ball carrier:
- he presents the easier side-on tackle
- and he can really only go one way, to the outside, unless he stops and then comes back inside. However, he then loses momentum.

⬤ Key factors to straight running are:
(i)   take the ball early
(ii) get on to a straight running line before receiving the pass
(iii) go back towards the passer, stepping into the pass
(iv) aim for the tackler's inside shoulder
(v)   the starting position is very important:
- outside foot forwards, i.e. the foot furthest from the ball. Immediately drive off that foot and hence towards the ball
- hips should be pointing down the field, parallel to the goal lines. Angled hips lead to angled running. This way, the hips are locked and it then makes it difficult to give the fall away pass.

Passing

⬤ General points.
(i)   Reasons for passing:
- to get the ball to a player in a better position
- to create space and stretch a defence
- to avoid being caught in possession with the risk of losing it.
(ii) Pass flat rather than deep to avoid losing ground.
(iii) Meet the ball early with hands and finger-tips. Set a target with your hands for the passer, at chest height.
(iv) Use the wrist in the motion of receiving and giving to adjust to an awkwardly received ball.
(v)   Pass with sympathy, i.e. with the correct weight behind it, so that the receiver can take the ball and give it on immediately.

⬤ The English method of passing.
(i)   When passing to the left, the ball is delivered when the right foot is in contact with the ground; when passing to the right, when the left foot is in contact with the ground.
(ii) The shoulders are at an angle to the would-be tackler and the receiver can see the passer's far shoulder.
(iii) The arms are swung across the body and the ball is aimed waist high.
(iv) As the pass is given, the hips sink and the passer falls away.

(v) Advantages are:
- it helps sell a dummy pass, and makes it easier to drive off at a different angle
- the fly-half can commit the loose forwards by putting them in two minds about an inside break
- because the shoulders are dipped, the ball is protected and it is possible to fend off the tackler with the side and shoulders.

(vi) Disadvantages are:
- the passer cannot support quickly because he is falling away from the direction of the pass
- if the receiver is taking the ball at waist height, his eyes are down and this limits his peripheral vision; he cannot scan in front of him
- running lines are angled and drifting outside the opposition, which makes it easier to defend against.

● The French method.
(i) The ball is delivered later but the body weight is more evenly distributed at the moment of releasing the ball.
(ii) Hips and shoulders are parallel to the goal lines.
(iii) The ball is taken at chest height.
(iv) Advantages are:
- it draws or fixes the opponent so he cannot drift across
- the receiver has his head and eyes up so he can scan
- he can break inside or outside
- he can support the pass quickly.

● The follow pass.
(i) The weight is on the foot nearer the receiver.
(ii) The passer follows the ball so he can support immediately.
(iii) Disadvantages are:
- the passer fails to draw his tackler
- it leads to drift and angled lines of running.

PLOYS

Principles

● The **purpose** of a tactical ploy is to:
(i) achieve a breakthrough and score. This does not happen often because defences are too well organised on the whole. If you manage to get through the first line of defence, generally the second line or third line prevents further progress

(ii) create second phase possession and then attack a disorganised defence. The point of the ploy might be to off balance
the defence momentarily and to get across the gain line. The
supporting forwards know where the attack is striking and
should get there first.

🏉 **Communication** is important.

(i) Firstly, among the three-quarters themselves so that each one
knows what the move is and therefore what will be expected
of him. Every three-quarter is involved in some way either in
a support role, a covering role or in the deception plan.

(ii) Secondly, the back row needs to know what is happening so
that if the three-quarters are switching and coming back
towards the forwards, at least the back row will not be running off towards the wings, but waiting for the cut back. A
signal could reverse the number of the three-quarter who is
making the strike, so that if '31!' is called the back row will
know that the right centre (no. 13) is the key man to follow.
Perhaps divide the field into four channels.

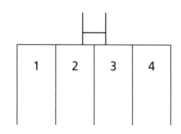

If there is a line-out in channel 1 and '4!' is called, then the
three-quarters are moving the ball as wide as they can. If '2!'
is called, the three-quarters are attacking the tail of the line-
out. If there is a scrum in channel 3 and '4!' is called, then
there is obviously an attack being launched down the narrow
side, perhaps with the full-back and the winger.

🏉 The **aim** of each move is to attack the **gaps** in the defending
three-quarter line with an **extra man**. Each three-quarter in the
diagram at the top of the next page is in a channel. How do we
create two-on-one situations, e.g. so that 10 is attacking 10 with
the help of an extra man, or 13 is attacking 12 with an extra man?

🏉 To **create the extra man**, each move in the end is based on
one of the following:

(i) a **switch of direction**

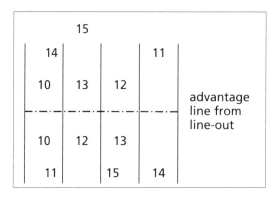

(ii) a **loop**
(iii) the **entry of an extra man from full-back or from the blind-side wing**.

◕ Success depends on having a **deception plan**. Decoy moves can involve:

(i)   body language, so that a player may look as though he is going to give a long pass when in reality he is going to give a short one to someone coming into the line close to him. Perhaps he may sell an early dummy and try to look as though he is going to have a go himself, when all he is trying to do is interest the defence before popping the ball to someone coming in close

(ii) a 'miss pass' is not a move in itself: it is just a means to move the ball further along the line more quickly. It can be part of the move to draw attention wide before passing the ball back inside

(iii) a dummy run is a good aid. The ball carrier could run across, dummying to players who are running straight, and therefore looking likely receivers of a pass. The blind-side winger or full-back are good players to use. They could run off the ball looking as though they are to be the primary strike players.

◕ A **fail safe** is important. If the move breaks down there must be someone covering any quick counter-attack by the opposition. Rarely, therefore, do we see both the full-back and the blind-side winger going into the line at the same time.

(i)   If the full-back goes into the line, then the blind-side winger covers across behind him.

(ii) If the blind-side winger goes in, the full-back is already covering.

(iii) If there is a scrum midfield and the full-back attacks to the right, the inside centre could cover deep since it is a long way to go for the left winger.

(iv) However, if you are prepared to take risks, trust each other's competence and believe in the move, then we can see both players in the line.

⬛ An **escape plan** is needed if things are going wrong and the ball is coming back slowly or untidily.

(i) **Cancel** and **kick**.

(ii) Employ a miss pass to move the ball wide if the full-back is coming in.

(iii) Turn the decoy dummy switch into the real strike and actually perform a switch to set up second phase, etc.

Loops

⬛ The player who is to loop gives a quick, flat pass.

(i) This pass should not be a fall away pass if he hopes to immediately support the new ball carrier, because he will be heading off in the wrong direction.

(ii) Neither should this pass be the follow pass. If this occurs it means that the looping player signals his intention straight away. He will also be heading off towards the touch line. He needs to delay his run.

⬛ The new ball carrier must create space behind him by accelerating on to the pass and getting beyond the looping player. The looping player can now get on a straight running line, if he has also delayed his run.

⬛ The ball carrier aims for the inside shoulder of the immediate tackler to draw him away from the gap where the looping player is heading. The ball carrier steps in but could switch to the outside shoulder of the defender just as he is giving the pass so that he can support the pass quickly and provide some protection for the ball and for the looping player.

⬛ The looping player should receive the pass on the shoulder of the ball carrier, and aiming for the gap in the defending line. The pass to him should be flat and sympathetic.

⬛ The passer should give the ball on:

(i) the outside shoulder from line-outs, i.e. facing the opposition. He has time from line-outs and the pass is not so pressurised

(ii) on the inside shoulder from scrums, i.e. he should turn inside showing the ball to the looping player all the time. There is

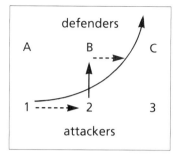

less time from scrums and the ball needs protection from the tackler.

Bringing in the extra man

🏉 Either the full-back or the blind-side winger can come into the line but it is unusual to have both in at the same time because if mistakes occur, cover is needed.

🏉 They can come in anywhere in the line provided that they do so at speed to receive a flat pass on the inside or outside of the passer. Often a deception plan is needed to avoid showing the opposition that the extra man is coming in.

🏉 The midfield will have to run with control. The extra man is starting some way behind the line and if that line is running at full pace, he will find it difficult to catch up.

🏉 The angle of entry does not always have to be the same.
(i) The blind-side winger tends to enter the line on an arc or running across. If he breaks through, his next pass should be almost immediate and to a player who is running straight.

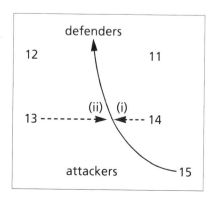

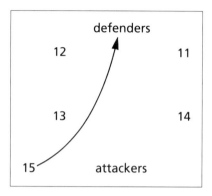

(ii) The full-back can come into the line running straight or across. Much depends on his intention and his starting position. He could start outside his winger and run back towards the midfield to check the drift defence, or he could start behind his midfield and run on an arc so that his run is somewhat disguised and also distracts the opposition midfield by crossing their line of vision.

Switches

⬤ There are several types of switch move, but there are factors common to them all.

(i) The ball carrier changes direction and runs across. The defender has to follow him and so a gap is created which the switching player will attack.

(ii) The switching player should decide when to change direction to receive the pass because the ball carrier will not have full vision of the defenders. The switching player will delay his run until the last possible moment to minimise the defenders' reaction time.

(iii) The pass will be screened from the opposition by the ball carrier's side and back. This will protect the ball in the event of a tackle being made at the moment the pass is being given. It also means that the ball is hidden from the defenders and a dummy switch is possible.

⬤ The **scissors** is where the switching player is running back towards his forwards. His angle of run is also across but the intention is to link up with his back row rather than his fellow three-quarters.

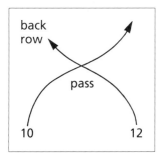

● The **switch** is where the angle of run is straight. The intention of the attacking player now is to link up with the three-quarters on the outside.

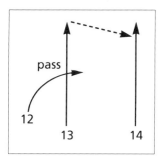

● The **outward switch** is where the switching player passes to the man outside him. The ball carrier then heads back, running across to hold the opposition on the inside. He then passes to the original ball carrier as he is running across, heading outside. This is similar to a loop, but the angles of run of both players make the difference.

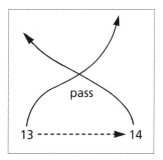

THE ORGANISATION OF DEFENCE

Defensive patterns

(Essentially, all defence is man-for-man. The question is: which man does a defender have to cover?)

● There are three basic defensive patterns.
(i) Man-for-man.
(ii) Drift defence.
(iii) Isolation.
Each is used from different situations.

● **Man-for-man.**
(i) Generally used from scrums and loose play.
(ii) It is easier for the defending fly-half to get up on his opposite number from a scrum.
(iii) Both centres and the fly-half go up fast and close together. They must be careful not to 'dog leg', i.e. the inside centre must not go up in front of the fly-half and the outside centre not before the inside centre. This can create gaps. Two centres working together, however, might employ it as a trap to entice an attempt at a break, and then close it down quickly.

Aim for the inside of your opposite number to drive him out – the hockey stick approach.

The fly-half could aim for the outside of the attacking fly-half to drive him back to the back row.

The chances are that a fly-half is right-footed, so on the left side of the field go up on his inside to force him to kick with his left foot. On the right-hand side of the field go up on his outside.

After the fly-half has passed, wait to see if anyone is cutting back into your zone and then cover behind the centres.
(iv) The open-side winger must first cover a kick by the fly-half or inside centre to his area of the field, and then go up quickly to tackle the player outside the outside centre. (This might be the full-back, or the winger, or the looping player.) He runs on an inverted arc to make the attacking winger go outside him, and also to maintain speed.
(v) If the blind-side winger comes into the midfield, the players all step in one.
(vi) The full-back covers across and takes the last man, i.e. the defending winger has taken out the full-back coming into the line at the usual place, outside the outside centre, but the

attacking full-back may have released his winger. The full-back must cover him.

(vii) There are problems inside your own 22-metre area. It is unlikely that the attack will kick here, so the full-back can stand wide and cover his opposite number if he comes into the line. Winger then covers winger.

(viii) However, some would like to see the defending full-back watch a blind-side attack from a scrum on the left. This leaves a potential overlap situation on the right, and a long distance to run to cover it.

(ix) The blind-side winger, from scrums, must watch for a break to his side, and also cover any kick into his area. After this he should cover deep behind the full-back.

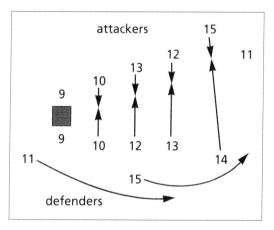

(x) The blind-side winger, from line-outs, covers across staying inside the ball. He tackles anyone who breaks through. There is no need for him to be on the touch line; he will be able always to get to the kick into the box or one aimed at touch. The best place for the winger to stand is near the fly-half and centre.

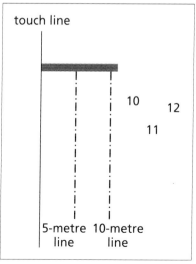

🏉 Midfield scrums present some difficulty, but generally what is employed is a man-for-man defence, with variations.

(i) If the attack 'packs' one side of the field with the fly-half and the centres, it is likely that it is going to attack the other side with its full-back.

Let the fly-half cover the full-back; the scrum-half must then cover the fly-half in case it goes to him attacking right.

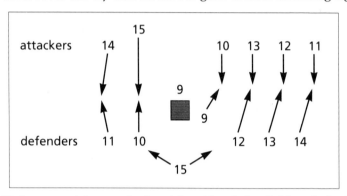

(ii) If the opposition pack the right side of the field and the ball goes to the fly-half, who then gives a long pass to the full-back going to the left, the scrum-half must cover this.

(iii) In both situations the defending full-back has to remain deep to cover any kick.

🏉 If a man-for-man defence is employed from line-outs, a key figure will be the blind-side winger.

(i) He should operate in a triangle with his fly-half and inside centre, and not be too far from them. If he stands just behind the fly-half and moves across behind the midfield, staying half a pass inside the ball, then he can cover any break-through that is made.

(ii) There is no need for him to be close to the touch line. If he is on the 15-metre line, then he should be able to get to any ball that is kicked into that area.

🏉 **Drift defence.**

(i) Generally employed from line-outs because it is difficult for the defending fly-half to get up on the attacking fly-half due to the distance involved, particularly if the fly-half passes immediately.

(ii) It can also be used from scrums on the left side of the field. Here the open-side flanker does not have to worry so much about a scrum-half break, and he can concentrate on the fly-half.

(iii) The main danger then is making sure that the attacking fly-half is covered by the open-side flanker from scrum and line-out. The no. 8 should cover him on the inside, to cover a break back by the fly-half.

(iv) If the attacking fly-half passes immediately, the defending fly-half should drift out on to the inside centre, the inside centre out on to the outside centre, and the outside centre out on to the full-back coming in between the winger and the outside centre. The extra man has been covered. If the extra man has not come into the line, then the attacking winger is crowded out.

(v) The midfield should approach the attackers very much on their inside, driving them out and making them run across the field, presenting the side-on tackle and reducing the space outside.

(vi) This leaves the blind-side winger and full-back to cover any kicks.

Inside your own 22-metre area it leaves the full-back to stand around the line-out, where his kicking and tackling skills might be useful. He could stand at fly-half or inside centre, allowing everyone to move out one.

(vii) This defence has been called 'An excuse not to go up quickly and tackle!' A quick drift, however, can be employed.

A 'one-out defence' is simply a drift defence, but the fly-half actually stands opposite the inside centre.

Isolation defence.

(i) Generally employed from set piece play.

(ii) The full-back is allowed to run when he comes into the line. The defending full-back has to cover him by getting across.

(iii) The other defenders should turn and isolate the full-back by cutting down his passing options.

(iv) It means that the fastest player on your side – the winger – stays on the fastest player on the other side, rather than coming in to take out the full-back who could release his winger on the overlap.

(v) It is a dangerous defence to utilise because the line has been penetrated. It is particularly difficult to employ near your own goal line.

(vi) It is usually used when the attack comes deep and the open-side winger and full-back are deep covering potential kicks. The winger is really stretched in getting up on to the extra player.

(vii) Communication is vital. Defenders should nominate the players they are covering, e.g. 'The full-back is mine!', etc.

⬤ Queensland defence.
(i)   Used from line-outs.
(ii) The blind-side winger stands outside the outside centre to cover the extra man.
(iii) The defending hooker has to cover the kick into the box vacated by this winger.
(iv) Dictate where the opposition play, but not through the centre. The fly-half will have to kick into the box or on the wide diagonal.

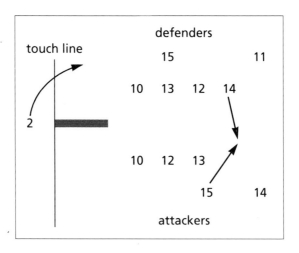

⬤ Zone defence.
(i)   Stay on the inside shoulder of the attacker. After he has passed the ball, do not sweep behind too early. Cover any change in direction. When the next ball carrier has passed on the ball, then sweep behind.
(ii) Take the man coming into your area. If the opposition switch, you should not.

⬤ If caught in a 2 v 1 situation, either:
(i)   back pedal and wait for cross cover to help
(ii) or stay inside both attackers, and drift (the ball carrier should accelerate into you to release the overlap).

COUNTER-ATTACK

General principles

📄 Possession from a poor opposition kick is good ball to use in attack because the defence tends to be disorganised. Some sides, however, will only counter-attack in the 15-metre area for safety reasons. There it is possible, if things go wrong, to run into touch with the ball or kick the ball into touch.

📄 A counter-attack usually pivots around 'the back three', i.e. the full-back and the two wingers. The pattern of movement depends on who receives the kick.

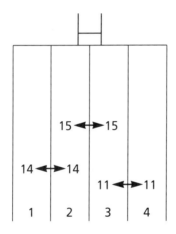

If the field is divided into four channels, then 14 operates in 1 and 2; 15 operates in 2 and 3; 11 operates in 3 and 4.

📄 Only counter when there is **time**, **space** and **support**.

📄 **Communication** and **decision-making** are vital. If the ball is in the air or on the ground, whoever is catching or gathering it will find it difficult to scan the field in front at the same time. One of the other back three players should slot in behind the ball receiver and make decisions for him, e.g. to pass, to kick high, or to kick to touch, etc.

📄 **Bring the ball forwards as quickly as possible.** Try to reduce the space between the ball and your own forwards quickly. It may be a long way to go back if things break down, and it is no good playing about while the opposition are coming up fast.

● The ball gatherer ought to off-load the ball to a player who is running, so that the counter-attack can gather pace. A player picking up the ball or receiving a high kick may have lost momentum. Also, the opposition is homing in on the ball gatherer and it may be possible to outflank these players by popping the ball up to a looping player or by giving a wide clearing pass.

● **Dummy to strength**, i.e. take the ball back in the direction of the kick to check the opposition forwards.

● **Switch to space**, i.e. move the ball now to the open areas where there are fewer defenders.

● If it is necessary to move the ball across the middle of the field, do so quickly. A player in midfield running with the ball will get caught if the opposition have been chasing up as they should.

● Midfield players must get back to support. Get between the ball and your own goal line. It may be preferable, however, to provide a shield of protection for the receiver of a high kick, the 'bomb'. Get back slowly, staying between the receiver and the chasers.

● 'Flair' is doing the unexpected successfully. It is the art of effective decision-making.

Simple counter-attacks

● To the **blind-side winger**.

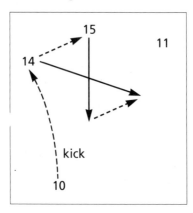

(i) In the diagram above, the opposition fly-half kicks into the box to the right winger (14). 14 gives a long clearing pass to the full-back (15). 15 **either** runs towards the forwards and gives a pass to 14 looping him, **or** runs into the open space to link up with 11.

(ii) 14 could run towards the fly-half (10) and do a switch with 15 who then kicks high down the touch line, **or** links with his own forwards.

● To the **full-back**.

(i) 15 runs back in the direction of the kick and switches with the blind-side winger (14). 14 then links with the open-side winger (11).

(ii) Much depends on where the ball lands for the full-back: if it is going to his left, i.e. towards his left winger, then he should be operating with him straight away and looking to his right winger to be in support of the attack he is launching.

(iii) He could be running to the open-side winger (11) and do a switch with him. However, since the ball is now heading back to trouble, 11 could do another switch with 14 to take the ball to the open again.

● To the **open-side winger**.

(i) If he can take the ball without losing momentum, then the open-side winger can immediately launch an attack against his opposite number, and look for help first from the full-back and then from the blind-side winger.

(ii) The ball may fall short, and he may be taking it as he is running in the direction of the kick. He then should do a switch with the full-back.

(iii) Similar to above, but he dummies his own full-back and switches with his blind-side winger so that there are two players running into the open space.

SKILLS

Individual evasive skills

A break

● An inside break is a side-step or a dummy, an acceleration and a change of direction inside the defender.

● An outside break generally relies on a swerve or a change of pace outside the defender.

● A half-break is when the ball carrier goes for a gap, perhaps committing two defenders and slipping the ball behind one of them to a support player accelerating into the space created.

🏉 The ball carrier who is making the break must have immediate support. He should be looking for this support and he should straighten the movement to deal with the cross cover.

🏉 The support should be close and coming from depth.

🏉 A tackle delays progress, and support must come in to take the ball and carry on the movement.

Swerving outside a defender: the right leg comes across the body; move the hips away from the defender; carry the ball in the arm further away from the tackler so that the free arm can fend him off

Evasion

- Run straight as a preliminary to beating a defender.

- Conceal speed by slowing down or running with control.

- A change of feet and direction necessitates good balance.

- The starting point of a movement is just beyond the defender's tackling range.

The **swerve**.
(i) Aim for the defender's inside shoulder.
(ii) There needs to be plenty of space between defender and attacker.
(iii) Swing away with a long first stride, which crosses over in front of the other leg. Lean away from the defender.
(iv) Control the pace and then accelerate.

The **side-step**.
(i) Shorten the strides.
(ii) Either hop on one leg and drive off the other . . .
(iii) . . . or push off at right angles to the direction of the run with a wide step.

The **dummy**.
(i) The arms swing out as if to pass. Look at the player for whom the pass is intended.
(ii) Bring the ball back.
(iii) The weight is on the inside foot, and the outside foot steps across the body to set off in the opposite direction.

Variation of pace.
(i) Run below top speed, then accelerate as the tackler is about to launch himself.
(ii) Lengthening and shortening the stride makes the tackler hesitate and puts him off balance.

Fend-off.
(i) Usually done when the tackler is approaching from an angle.
(ii) The arm is bent and then straightened as the hand pushes off the tackler's body (his head or shoulders).
(iii) Hold the ball in the far arm.

Breaking the tackle.
(i) Turn the hip and shoulder into the tackler to bounce him off.
(ii) Protect the knee with a bent arm, elbow down.
(ii) Keep the legs driving and maintain a low body position.
(iv) One shoulder tends to lead. Use the forearm and shoulder to fend off.

Tackling

General points.
(i) Effective tackling means flooring the ball carrier so that he has to release the ball and is momentarily out of the game.

(ii) The tackler should aim to end up on top of the tackled player so that he can be up and away again before the tackled player.

(iii) Use your shoulder when making contact, but the power comes through the body from the legs. Keep a straight back and keep the chin up.

(iv) Use your body weight to pull down and use your hands to hold on to whatever you have grabbed.

(v) Crashing front tackles tend to be performed by centres in an area where the players are running flat out at each other; also, by a winger on a full-back who has come into the line.

(vi) Side tackles are usually carried out by outside centres or wingers when their opponents are trying an outside break. Covering wingers and full-backs also use this tackle, as well as the rear tackle.

● Front tackles.

(i) The running front tackle (or 'crash tackle') involves getting up on the ball carrier as quickly as possible to cut down his options and make him do what *you* want him to do.

(ii) When you launch yourself, your aim really depends on your own size and that of your opponent:
– aim low, between the ankles and the knees, if your opponent is too strong to be tackled around the hips. Then drive upwards. If possible, keep your feet on the ground
– aim between the knees and the stomach if your opponent looks weaker or ungainly, or if he is momentarily distracted as he receives the pass.

(iii) Timing your run is important. Get within tackling range quickly. Arrive in control and accelerate into the tackle.

(iv) Keep an eye on the ball and an eye on your opponent to make sure that he is not changing the angle of his run. Try to tackle him as he receives the ball.

(v) With the standing front tackle it is difficult to knock the ball carrier back because *he* has all the momentum:
– crouch low with a wide base and with knees bent
– drive in at the ball carrier's thighs.

(vi) If you are unlikely to knock him over due to his size, then take the impact on your shoulder and roll backwards, absorbing the impact, twist and end up on top.

(vii) You can also side-step to one side and as he draws level, drive into him from the side.

● The side tackle.

(i) Aim at the thighs. Hit with the shoulders.

(ii) Drive from the legs. Squeeze with the arms.

(iii) The head should be on the opponent's backside.

🏉 The rear tackle.
(i) Aim for the waist or top of the thigh, and slide down.
(ii) Hold on rather than drive in.

Ball retention

🏉 When a three-quarter is tackled, it is important that he retains possession and makes the ball available for his support.

🏉 The ball carrier must try to stay on his feet by using his foot-work to make the tackler take him from one side. He can then use the tackler as support, and rest an elbow on his back while swinging around behind the tackler's head to distribute the ball.

🏉 If the ball carrier cannot stay on his feet, he must present the ball properly by placing it on the ground so that his support can pick up and carry on.

🏉 Three-quarters support three-quarters. Each player is responsible for seeing the ball safely through the next pair of hands. If the player is tackled, the person who passed him the ball must go in and help secure the ball. He should not stand by and wait for forwards to arrive. He has three choices:
(i) to go in and seal off the ball, and wait for the forwards to carry on the maul
(ii) to rip out the ball and go on running, or pop it up to someone running faster than he is
(iii) to pick up the ball, continue running or pop it up to someone else.

🏉 The tackled player must decide where his support is coming from, and turn towards it. He should look inside for his back row, and outwards for another three-quarter.

🏉 The tackled player must also decide what he is able to do with the ball. If his arms are free, it may be possible to make a pass. If his arms are pinned, he must hold on and wait for assistance.

🏉 The supporting three-quarter should assess the situation and realise that the tackled player may be able to pass. If that is pos-sible, he should realise that the pass will not be a long one. He will have to come in close and be running on to a very short pass.

Retaining the ball in the tackle: keep a low, wide base; move the ball away from the tackler; the left arm and shoulder fend off the defender

Kicking

⬤ General points: attacking kicks.

(i) The high (or 'bomber') kick into the box in front of the forwards. The chasers would be the winger and the inside centre. One tries to get his hands to the ball; the other acts as sweeper. This pincer movement also helps to prevent a counter-attack.

(ii) The high kick towards the posts. The chasers would be both centres, with similar roles to above.

(iii) The diagonal kick to the open side behind the winger. This is best done by the inside centre because the winger tends to be moving up on his opposite number after the fly-half has passed the ball. There should be more space behind if the kick is thus delayed.

(iv) The chip kick over the midfield can be made by either the fly-half or the inside centre. It is made when the opposition is coming up very quickly. But the line must surge through to repossess the ball.

(v) The grubber kick through gaps in the opposing midfield, with the subsequent chase, can also be effective.

⬤ Kicks at goal and re-starts are:

(i) the place kick

(ii) the drop kick.

⬤ The punt: the diagonal (or touch line) kick.

(i) The ball should be held at an angle of 45° to the axis of the foot.

(ii) The right hand should be under the ball at the end nearer you. The left hand should be under the ball at the end further from you. This is for a kick with the right foot. Reverse everything for a kick with the left. You provide a 'gate' with your hands through which you kick.

(iii) Hold the ball about waist high, and an arm's length away from the body.

(iv) Place the ball on a 'shelf', and hit the centre of the ball with the top of the foot. There is a magic triangle at the base of the leg where it meets the ankle. The ball should still be at an angle, and it is this angle which gives the ball spin.

(v) Point the toe downwards.

(vi) Follow through for greater control and power. A stab at the

*Punting the ball: left hand to right foot; left shoulder closed; head ►
down; kicking leg follows through*

ball without the follow through means it is difficult to control direction.

(vii) Keep your head down and the body over the ball. Your left shoulder should be forward. Left hand to right foot.

🏈 The high kick into the box or towards the posts.
(i) The ball can be held upright with the hands on either side of it.
(ii) Drop the ball on to the foot so that you kick the point of the ball.
(iii) All other principles for the punt apply here.

🏈 The chip kick.
(i) The long axis of the ball should be at right angles to the foot.
(ii) The toes tend to be pointed up.
(iii) Lean forwards and ensure a high knee lift so that there is no loss of momentum and that you are immediately into your running stride again. Sometimes there is body lean to the side away from the kicking foot.

🏈 The grubber kick.
(i) The ball is held upright with the hands on either side of it. The ball should roll end over end.
(ii) Hit the ball before it reaches the ground with the top, inside or outside of the foot, depending on preference. Strike the upper half of the ball.
(iii) Lean forwards so that there is little loss of momentum.
(iv) Only kick into gaps. Retrieve the ball when it bounces up.

🏈 The drop kick.
(i) Drop the ball upright but slightly tilted towards you, so that when it bounces it should be bouncing backwards.
(ii) As it hits the ground, use your instep or the inner side of the top of your foot to kick the ball.

🏈 The place kick.
(i) Either tee up the ball with sand or earth, or put the ball in a hole made in the ground with the heel of your boot. Better still, use a manufactured kicking tee.
(ii) Place your left foot alongside the ball and your right foot behind it. Walk backwards to measure your run up, e.g. three strides back and two to the side for the round-the-corner kick.
(iii) Contact is made with the instep or with the top of the big toe.
(iv) The non-kicking foot should end up alongside the ball.
(v) Keep your eyes on the ball and do not lift the head too early.

Scrum-half kicking into the box: face the touch line; hit the centre of the ball with the top of the foot; keep the left shoulder tight; follow through with the kicking leg

Scrum-half pass: stay low; keep the right foot back and pointing towards the receiver, thus unlocking the hips and keeping the right knee out of the way

(vi) Hold your left arm out for balance. Follow through. The kicking foot should return alongside the non-kicking foot if you are well balanced.

Scrum-half passes

Dive pass.
(i) The foot nearer the scrum/line-out is behind the ball and pointing towards the line of the pass.
(ii) The weight is on the balls of the feet, and the knees are bent.
(iii) The shoulders and body are over the ball.
(iv) The ball is scooped and swept in one movement.

(v) Move forwards on to the other foot, then drive off it high and forwards.
(vi) Straighten the body. The hands on the ball are now pointing towards the feet. The arms are held back as long as possible.
(vii) Cushion the body on the hands after releasing the ball so as to get up quickly.

🏉 Standing spin pass.
(i)   If passing to the right, the left foot should be behind the ball and the right foot close by. The weight is on the left foot.
(ii) The head and body are over the ball, with knees bent.
(iii) Transfer the weight to the right foot as a step is taken. The right foot extends along the line of the pass and points in the direction of the pass.
(iv) For speed and whip, whip the left leg behind for the follow through. Include plenty of hip action.
(v)   Keep the chin down, and the head and shoulders parallel to the ground.
(vi) Sweep the ball away from the ground with a quick flick of the wrists.
(vii) A wide step is for power; a short step is for speed. A short step will allow the scrum-half to support quickly.

🏉 *Note*   The 'Dave Loveridge pass'. Occasionally Loveridge's hands were crossed when reaching for the ball, e.g. when he approached the ball from the right to pass to the right, his right hand would go to the far side of the ball, beyond the left hand. The left hand would be under the ball and as the pass was made, the left hand would come around behind the right hand and eventually appear on top of the ball. This gave the ball extra spin.

🏉 Common faults in the standing spin pass:
(i)   poor positioning of the feet at the pick-up and step
(ii) knees not bent
(iii) standing up prematurely
(iv) picking up the ball and winding up the pass.

🏉 Reverse pass.
(i)   Get both feet and the body between the ball and the opposition.
(ii) The thumbs are on top of the ball and the hands are to the front of it.
(iii) The head and shoulders remain forward over the ball as the eyes glance backwards over the right arm.
(iv) Follow through with the arms and the fingers as the body and the ball go in opposite directions.

● Pivot pass: standing or diving.
(i)   Face touch with your weight on the right foot, i.e. the foot nearest the ball.
(ii) Transfer the weight to the left foot as the body swivels around.
(iii) Note the key factors to the standing spin pass and the dive pass.

● Poor presentation of the ball to the scrum-half is dealt with as follows.
(i)   If the ball is rolling towards you, trap it on the ground with one hand to stop it, and then pass.
(ii) If the ball is in the air, say off the top of the line-out, and you want to pass to your left but the ball is coming down to your left, then you must move your feet quickly so that the ball is coming down to your right. This eliminates the need for a wind-up pass because your hands and arms are now in the right position to take and give immediately.

PART II

EXERCISES FOR INDIVIDUAL AND POSITIONAL SKILLS

HANDLING

In pairs with a ball. Stand opposite each other, 1–2 metres apart. Keep passing all the time. Perhaps include jogging on the spot.

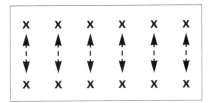

(i) 'Change!' Quickly swop positions.
(ii) 'Down on knees!' Both kneel. Face each other. Keep passing.
(iii) 'Sitting!' Face each other. Keep passing.
(iv) Sitting back-to-back and passing over head.
(v) Lying down, head-to-head. Keep passing.
(vi) Lying down, feet-to-feet. Keep passing.
(vii) Standing – try different passes, e.g. ball around back, headed, etc.
(viii) Get further apart and give long passes.
(ix) Leaning slightly forwards, give a pass to the left and then to the right of the catcher so that he has to reach for it with one arm and pull it in.

As above, but moving about according to instructions. Maintain the distance between the pairs and keep passing. Keep facing each other.
(i) Calls of 'Left!', 'Right!', 'Forwards!', 'Backwards!', 'Diagonal left!', 'Diagonal right!'.

(ii) Give visual signals.
(iii) One player moving backwards, roll the ball forwards to the oncoming player who scoops it up and gives a quick pass back.
(iv) As above, but *place* the ball.
(v) One player gives an overhead pass, and the other gives a low pass from below his knees.
(vi) A soft punt and a quick return pass.
(vii) Always give a pass which is parallel to the touch line, but the player going backwards must dodge about and his partner must stay opposite him by reacting accordingly – always a mirror image.

◗ As the last exercise, but staggered. Close up the distance between each pair.

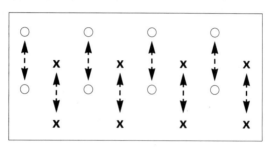

(i) The os remain stationary and the xs move left or right, passing through the gaps.

◗ In pairs with a ball. Keep passing as everyone jogs around in two long files.

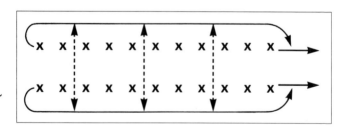

(i) On call of 'Go!' the back pair run to the front on the outside, giving a nominated number of long passes between the gaps.
(ii) Each pair gets wider and the back pair have to run down the middle. Keep the eyes open.
(iii) Swap sides occasionally.
(iv) The ball is passed over the head to the player behind. When

the ball gets to the end of each file, the ball carrier runs to the front and the sequence starts again. Add more balls to each line.

◖ In fours with a ball. Stand 3–4 metres apart in the shape of a square. Pass the ball around the grid quickly.

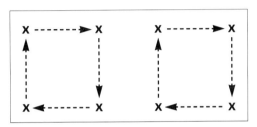

(i)   On call of 'Change!', change the direction of the passes.
(ii) Add a second ball. **Turn the head and the eyes quickly. Emphasise eye contact with the receiver.**
(iii) Add a third and then a fourth ball.
(iv) One ball. After passing, do a press-up or any other nominated exercise.
(v)   On a given signal, three react by moving to the ball carrier. Two bind over the top and the ball carrier distributes to the third player. Devise other reactions.
(vi) Get closer inside the grid, and after each pass touch the corner cone behind you or run around it.

◖ Groups of four with a ball, 3–4 metres apart in the shape of a square. Two to run backwards and two to run forwards.

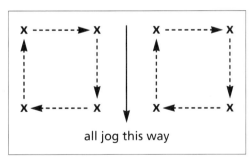

all jog this way

(i)   Keep passing around that square.
(ii) The pair running forwards put pressure on the pair running backwards by almost running so hard as to bump into them.
(iii) When the second player running backwards receives his pass, he puts the ball down for the next player running forwards to pick up and give a quick pass to his partner, etc.

(iv) As above but *roll* it back.
(v) Now a *lob*.

🏉   Any number, e.g. 5, 8 or 10. Players in the middle are stationary, and receive and give passes. Players at either end must give each of the middle players a pass and run on to a return pass.

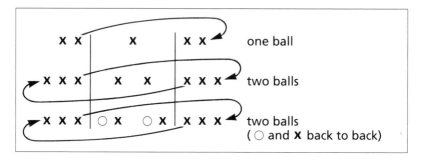

(i) Ordinary passes – be sympathetic.
(ii) The first return pass from the middle player is placed for the running player to pick up. If there is a second pass to be made and returned, do it as normal.
(iii) As above, but *roll* the ball for the first return pass.
(iv) Now *lob* the ball.
(v) Now *bounce* the ball on the ground.
(vi) Now give a difficult but receivable pass.

🏉   Everyone in a large grid running about in any direction. Avoid contact. Use plenty of balls.
(i) Pass to anyone. Emphasise **eye contact with catcher** and **hands up ready**.
(ii) 'Short passes only!' Only give a pass to someone who is near you.
(iii) 'Long passes!' – go wider to receive a pass. Only pass to someone a long way from you.
(iv) Ball around body/around one leg/figure of eight around both legs/any combination before passing.
(v) 'Ball down!' – ball carrier puts ball down on command, goes to pick up another one and starts passing again until the next order.
(vi) Any type of pass. Be clever, e.g. one-handed around back, overhead (backwards and forwards).
(vii) Pass by bouncing the ball off any part of the body, e.g. elbow, foot, head, shoulder.
(viii) As (v), but someone falls on the ball, gets up and passes.
(ix) 'Bounce!' – bounce the ball on the ground and collect it.

(x)   'Lob!' – lob the ball over someone's head and run around to catch it.

These exercises can also be done in this grid in small groups of three to five players working together but moving about the same grid all the time.

(xi)   1 puts ball down; 2 steps over, bends and pops it up to 3, etc.

(xii) 1 puts ball down; 2 falls and secures it; 3 steps over and lifts it to 1, etc.

(xiii) 1 throws ball in air; 2 goes up to collect it and distributes to 3 or taps it to 3, etc.

(xiv) Pass, pass, go in and take, and pop out.

(xv)   Pass, pass and 2 goes in and turns the ball carrier for 3 to wrestle the ball clear.

(xvi) 2 passes. Then the ball carrier is decked by pulling him over the hip. Ball carrier tries to keep the ball on his own side when he places it.

(xvii) 1 throws ball over his head into the air; 2 catches and steps into 1 who has now turned and become a defender; 3 goes in to help.

◗ Two single files facing each other, four to eight in each.

(i)   One ball. The receiver comes out and meets the ball carrier in the middle, i.e. one from each end run at the same time to meet in the middle. Use soft, pop passes. Players then join the other line.

(ii)   Add more balls so a continuous stream of players is running. Only pass to someone who does not have a ball.

(iii) As (i) but lob the ball well before meeting.

(iv)   Roll the ball well before meeting.

(v)   Two balls, one at each end. Put the ball 2 metres out, run and pick up the other one and pop it to the player waiting at the head of the line.

(vi)   As (v), but roll the ball to the side, run after it and fall on it, get up and hand on.

(vii) Start with the ball on the ground 2 metres out. Pop it up to a support player who runs on and puts the ball down in front of the other line.

(viii) Introduce a loop so that the player who pops the ball up to the support player now loops him to receive a pass.

(ix)   As (i), but let the receiver run slightly past so that the ball carrier has to pass backwards.

(x)   As (ix), but lob the ball over the shoulder so the receiver is running on to a high ball.

(xi)   As (vii), but the support player drives into the ball carrier, rolls off, then puts down.

🏉 All these exercises are similar to the very first one except that they are in opposite files. The players can stand closer; they can give different passes; they can give a mixture of passes; the passer can then run to join the opposite line and run back to re-join his own line.

🏉 Union Jack exercise.

1	2	3
8		4
7	6	5

Pass to left/right and run to opposite point, i.e. 1 to 5 and vice versa; 2 to 6; 3 to 7; 4 to 8.

(i)   Coach shouts 'Change!' and the ball is sent around in the opposite direction. The first pass will be a long one. A space has been vacated.

(ii)   Pass and follow, so 1 passes to 2 and runs to 2; 2 to 3; 3 to 4, etc.

(iii)   Two balls starting in opposite corners.

(iv)   2 now runs to 4; 4 to 6; 6 to 8; 8 to 2, while the corner men follow the ball around the grid by running to each corner in turn, i.e. 1 goes to 3; 3 to 5; 5 to 7.

(v)   Alternate passes, e.g. roll ball followed by quick pass off ground, followed by roll ball, etc.

🏉 In groups of four. Start on the goal line and jog to the 22-metre line. Keep passing. When the line gets to the 22-metre line it starts running backwards back to the goal line. In the meantime, the other waves will be coming through them.

When the line gets to the goal line, it starts to jog forwards again to the 22-metre line, avoiding the other waves coming back. Continuous running and passing for a specified time. This helps develop peripheral vision.

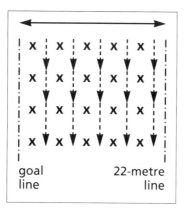

Avoid contact. Do not drop the ball. Do not pass to a 'marked' player or have the ball intercepted by bouncing it off a player from another line! Keep the distance between each wave.

Progression (i): each wave turns on the 22-metre line and comes back facing the other waves. Start to find gaps and accelerate through them.

Progression (ii): perform loops somewhere in the line, or switches at the end. Miss one, followed by an inside pass, followed by a miss one.

Progression (iii): all passes from below the knees; from above the head; ball to circle the body before being passed.

In groups of four. Running and passing the length of the field. Each player is numbered off and each group is partnered off with another group. Run down the 15-metre channel on either side of the pitch.

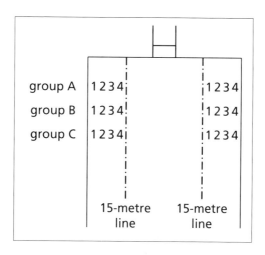

As the groups move in waves down the pitch, the coach calls out any number from 1 to 4. The nominated player has to run hard to join the group his own has been paired with so that the numbers in each group stay the same but the personnel keeps changing. **Back row in support of a wide attack.**

Call out two, then three, then four numbers so that eventually the group will just be swapping channels.

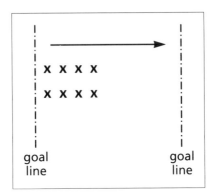

One ball with the first player, who is standing on the goal line. The other players are spread out in a file heading towards the other goal line. The ball has to be passed through every pair of hands. No-one may run with the ball. Pass and then run to the end of the line. The first team to get the ball to the other end of the pitch is the winner.

Development: introduce a second ball. Each ball has to be passed through every pair of hands. There are to be no cut-out passes. Pass, then run to the end of the line.

Form a circle of five to eight players. One ball. Pass to anyone in the circle and follow the pass, thus taking the place of the player who has just received the ball, passed it and followed.

In a circle.
(i)   Bend the knees and lean forwards. Roll the ball along the ground across the circle. The receiver collects and rolls the ball along the ground anywhere across the circle. Keep stretching.
(ii) Grub kick to anyone across the circle.
(iii) On tip toes and stretching up. Lob the ball to anyone in the circle.
(iv) Combination of different types of pass to anyone across the circle.
(v)   Introduce more balls.

(vi) Lie down with the feet inwards, or stand up and face outwards. Keep passing.

⬤ Group of five with one ball. 1 faces the other four who are in a straight line.

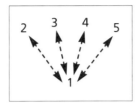

(i) 1 passes the ball to each in turn and the others pass the ball back. When the ball is received from 5, 1 puts the ball down and joins the line at the beginning while 5 takes his place. All shuffle along and the sequence starts all over again until everyone has been in 1's position.

(ii) Try different passes and different body positions.

⬤ Teams of four starting at one goal line and facing down the pitch, either one behind the other or side by side. On the signal there will be a race to the other goal line. A pass has to be made on the 22-metre line, the half-way line and the far 22-metre line. The last ball carrier must score. The first team to score is the winner. Change positions in the line-up and go four times so that everyone runs the same distance.

PASSING

Technique

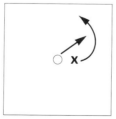

⬤ Evader (x), with a ball, keeps 1 metre away from the chaser (o) for one minute; x tries to lose o. **Carry the ball in two hands.**

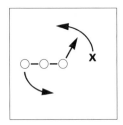

⬤ Three in tag. *x* tries to touch the end player with a ball. The others try to prevent it by getting in the way. **Carry the ball in two hands.**

⬤ Each file is 2 metres apart. Pass and follow and join the end of the opposite file. **Hands behind the ball. Only thumb showing to the receiver.**
Development: put the ball on the ground between your legs. Reach behind the knees to the ball and push it up towards the receiver. There should be little pick-up and no back-swing. **Push the ball. Use wrists and fingers.**

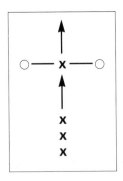

⬤ *x*s line up and take it in turns to walk between the two *o*s, who have outstretched arms. One of them is holding a ball. *x* reaches for the ball and hands it on to the other *o*. **Reach for the ball and take it early. Set a target with your hands.**
Progression (i): have two *x*s and set the *o*s wider apart. Jogging. A slight modification of the position of *o*s and this practice can be used to build up a three-quarter line.
Progression (ii): in threes, running and passing. Middle player keeps on a straight running line.

⬤ In threes with a ball. Static. 1 passes to 2 who then passes to 3; 2 does a press-up quickly and gets up to receive a pass from

3 to give to 1. After each pass, he does a press-up or similar exercise to speed up his reactions.

Progression: two balls. 2 throws a ball into the air and 1 passes him another. He must get the ball away to 3 and catch the one he threw in the air, etc.

Weight of pass

🏉 Grid or channels. Groups of four. Lateral passing. The two middle players stand close together and the two at each end stand wide (*see* diagram below). Each player keeps on a straight running line to maintain the same gaps as they run and pass. **Hard and soft passes. Vary the weight of pass.**

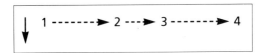

🏉 Grid or channels. In fours. 1 passes to 2 who gives a long pass to 4, missing out 3. 4 passes to 3 who gives a long pass to 1, missing out 2. (*See* diagram below.)

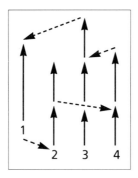

The throw-away or fade pass (*see* top of next page). Static defenders (o). 2 runs with the ball on a straight running line all the time. Before entering interception range, 1 fades away from 2 to the far side of the defender as 2 passes to him, weighting the pass correctly. After passing this defender, 1 passes the ball back to 2 and then gets on the correct running line straight towards the next defender. The same sequence happens again.

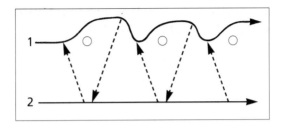

The short or cut-in pass. As above. 2 keeps on a straight run-ning line but 1 cuts in towards the pass and inside the defender as 2 passes to him. He again passes the ball back to 2 and resumes a straight running line at the next defender.

Progression: combine these last two exercises. 1 calls for a short or fade pass, as he wishes, and 2 has to react correctly.

Running lines

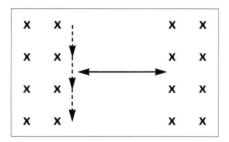

One ball only. Relay. One wave passes the ball along the line to the end player as they jog/run forwards. When the ball is in the end player's hands, the wave opposite comes out to meet the other wave and the ball is popped up to that line, who now pass it along to the end player. When it is in his hands, the next wave comes out, etc. **Set a target for the ball with your hands. Run straight. The end player hangs back to come from depth to accelerate on to a flat pass.**

(i)   Reduce the distance between the starting positions to put pressure on the passing. Increase the distance and the ball can be passed along the line twice.

(ii) 1 passes to 2. He then either loops him to receive a return pass, or he waits for 2 to pass to 3 and then appears outside 3 to receive a pass and give one to 4.

(iii)   1 passes to 2 who passes to 3. 3 passes to 4 and loops him.

(iv)   1 passes to 2, 2 passes to 3, 3 passes to 4, and then the end player comes in at an angle and does an outward switch with player 3.

(v)   1 passes to 3, missing out 2. 3 runs back at an angle to do an outward switch with 2 who then passes to 4. It could be also a miss pass, followed by the missed out player looping.

(vi)   Player 1 misses out 2 and passes to 3. 3 passes back inside to 2 who passes straight to 4, missing out 3.

(vii)   1 passes to 3. 1 and 2 both loop 3. 3 passes either to 1 or 2 and the ball is passed down the line.

(viii)   1 passes to 2 who runs across to do a dummy switch with 3, and passes to 4 running straight.

(ix)   1 passes to 2 who passes to 3. 3 and 4 do a switch. 4 must now make sure he gets the ball to the end player of the oncoming wave.

(x)   2 does a dummy switch with 3 and a switch with 4.

(xi)   1 passes to 2. 2 and 3 run across and 4 runs behind them to take a switch from 2.

(xii)   Pass and loop. Everyone loops to the end to receive another pass.

(xiii)   1 passes to 2 who switches with 3. 3 then switches with 1, who takes it out again and gives a flat pass to 4 who is running straight. A double switch.

(xiv)   Vary the type of pass:
- from below the knees
- from above the head, directed down to the chest
- lobbed
- ordinary pass followed by tap pass
- other combinations of passes.

⬤ This passing can be carried out down channels in waves or across grids.

⬤ Fours in a grid. 1 passes to 2 and then tries to stop the winger from scoring (two-handed touch or proper tackle) by running behind the line to catch him from behind.
Progression: tackler runs in front of the line and tries to stop the three attackers from scoring.

⬤ 4 starts on the goal line and 1, 2 and 3 start 5 metres in front. (*See* diagram at top of next page.) On the signal they all race to the half-way line. 4 tries to catch 1, 2 and 3 with the ball.

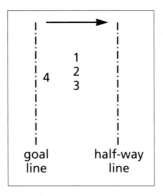

1, 2 and 3 must keep passing and must not get caught nor allow 4 to get in front of them. They cannot run with the ball in their hands for longer than a distance of 3 metres.

A grid 15/20 metres square. Each player in each team is numbered off. Give each team a letter. On the signal, the nominated group runs across the grid to the opposite side while passing.
Progression (i): call two groups out at the same time, then three and finally all four.
Progression (ii): the ball starts with the player at the extreme right. After passing, he loops the entire line. Include any loop or switch as they cross the grid.
Progression (iii): as one line crosses the grid, call out players from the other grid lines to become defenders and stop them, e.g. if group A is attacking, call out 1 from group B to stop them or call out all the 1s to interfere.

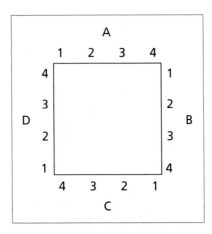

The Auckland exercises

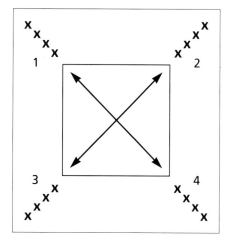

⬤ A ball in each corner of the grid. Players run to the opposite corner, i.e. 1 to 4 and vice versa, and 2 to 3 and vice versa. A test of peripheral vision and reaction speed. The running and handling must be done at pace. The more players in each corner, the longer the rest period for each.

Passing

(i) One from each corner runs and hands the ball on to the next player in the opposite corner.
(ii) The receiver now runs out 2 metres to meet the ball carrier.
(iii) The receiver now starts to run at the same time as the ball carrier so that they meet in the middle. There will be eight players in the middle of the grid at any one time. Try to avoid contact. Make sure the ball gets to the player for whom it is intended. Call for the ball. Establish eye contact with the receiver.
(iv) **Two** from each corner come out. The ball carrier passes to the support player once they have crossed midway. The support player hands on to the next pair waiting.
(v) As above, but the ball carrier makes a pass to his partner **before** midway, and receives a pass back **after** midway.

Ball on the ground

(i) One from each corner runs across the grid and puts the ball down 2 metres out from the opposite corner. The next player runs to pick it up, crosses the grid and puts the ball down 2 metres out for the next one to pick up, etc.

(ii) One from each corner puts the ball down 2 metres out from his own corner as he crosses the grid. He pops up the other ball left in the opposite corner to the next player waiting in the corner. He puts the ball down 2 metres out and crosses to pop up the ball left in the opposite corner. No ball crosses the grid, therefore. It is put down and popped up in the same corner each time.

(iii) The ball carrier still puts the ball down 2 metres out from his own corner, but he now falls on the ball in the opposite corner and quickly gets up with it to hand on to the next player.

(iv) The ball carrier rolls the ball to the waiting player from about 4 metres out, i.e. just past midway in the grid. The waiting player comes out to meet the ball to collect it on the run.

(v) As (iv), but now the player falls on the rolling ball, collects, gets up and rolls the ball for the next player.

Evasion

(i) Position cones as gates to be stepped through. *x* heads for one cone and then side-steps through the gate comprised of two cones, before making his way across the grid.

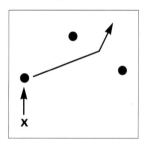

(ii) Put a tackle bag or a large cone 2 metres out from each corner. Side-step the one in your corner and in the opposite corner.

SCRUM-HALF PASSES AND POSITIONAL PLAY

All exercises can be adapted to practise the four basic scrum-half passes: standing, pivot, dive, reverse.

✏ Each receiver runs on to the pass, returns the ball and re-joins the end of the queue. (*See* top of page 60.)

Scrum-half pass: the right foot points at the receiver; the right knee and hip are unlocked; stay low; the head and shoulders point in the direction of the pass

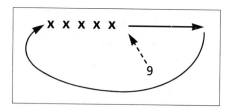

🏉 (i) C rolls the ball to 9 who passes to A. A returns the ball to C. D then rolls the ball to 9 who passes to B. B returns the ball to D.

(ii) C to 9 and 9 to B. D to 9 and 9 to A.

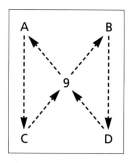

🏉 (i) C feeds 9 who passes to A. 9 runs to A who feeds 9. 9 passes to B then follows the ball, etc.

(ii) Vary the feed, e.g. 9 has to rip the ball away, or A, B or C rolls or places the ball, or gives awkward passes.

(iii) A, B or C could shout 'Left!' or 'Right!' to check 9's responses.

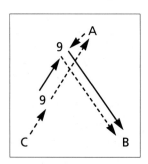

🏉 (i) 9 passes to C, who puts the ball on the ground. 9 follows the pass and now passes to A, who puts the ball on the ground. 9 follows his pass and now passes to B. From B his next pass is diagonal to C, who now becomes scrum-half while the original 9 returns to his own corner. Vary the way the ball is distributed to the scrum-half.

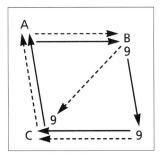

(ii) Each pass is a pivot pass. The scrum-half approaches the ball by running to the centre of the grid first and as he picks up the ball his back should be facing the receiver of the pass.

🏉 A and C have a ball each. C feeds 9, who passes to D. 9 runs to A, who feeds him. 9 passes to B. 9 runs to D, who feeds him. 9 passes to C. 9 runs to B, who feeds him. 9 passes to A. 9 runs to C, who feeds him, etc.

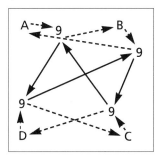

If there are six players, place one in the middle of the grid. 9 goes to A, B, C and D in turn and passes to the middle player. After each pass 9 goes to the middle player to give a pass to the next corner of the grid.

🏉 Dive pass: roll ball away, follow, collect and dive-pass. Get behind the ball, drive from the legs, and flick the wrists.

🏉 Four types of pass. Coach calls: 'Left standing!'; 'Right pivot!'; 'Left reverse!', etc.
Progression (i): xs go in pairs so that the fly-half passes to a support player. Then xs go in threes. The xs who are working together come from the same line.
Progression (ii): one fly-half on each side kicks the ball high. The rest in pairs or threes chase and recover possession.

🏉 A, B, C, D, E and F distribute the ball to 9. 9 passes to B and runs to receive a return pass. 9 passes to C. This time he kicks to D. After receiving a pass from F, he breaks to score.

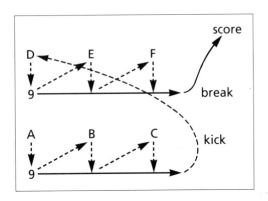

In pairs.

(i) Five to ten balls. Keep the feet still if possible. Maintain a wide base and bent knees. Do not come up between each pass. The left foot is next to the ball. This exercise develops wrists, fingers and thighs.

(ii) Use the left hand only to develop wrists and fingers.

(iii) Quick hands developed by quickly passing a number of balls to the fly-half, almost without looking. The fly-half puts each ball down immediately because there should be another on its way.

Scrum ball

(i) 1 v 1 scrummaging. 9 feeds the scrum. The ball is hooked and 9 passes to 10. 9 either loops outside 10 or receives an inside pass. (*See* diagram below.)

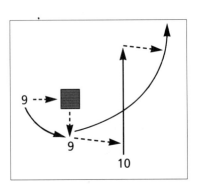

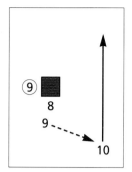

(ii) Ball at no. 8's feet. 8 controls the ball in various ways (forwards, back, pick-up). 9 passes to 10 or breaks with 8.

(iii) Introduce an opposing 9 who becomes active when 8 or 9 touches the ball. (*See* diagram above.)

Line-out ball

2 throws to jumper 4, who feeds 9 in different ways. 9 passes to 10. The opposing 2 and 8 counter in a pincer movement.

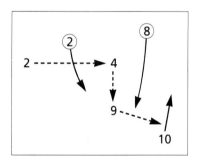

1 feeds 9 with line-out ball. 9 passes to 2 and follows pass. 2 feeds 9 line-out ball. 9 passes to 1 and follows pass, etc.

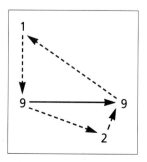

Ruck/maul ball

🏉   9 runs to each ball and passes to 10. Repeat the passing off the other hand.

Progression (i): number each ball; the coach calls which ball is to be played next. This involves some retreating and re-adjustment of alignment.

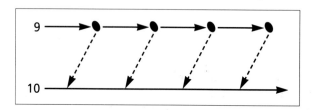

Progression (ii): fly-half communication. He decides where he wants the ball passed, and shouts 'Wide left/right!' or 'Short left/right!', etc.

🏉   As above. Use two fly-halves. Running off ruck or maul.

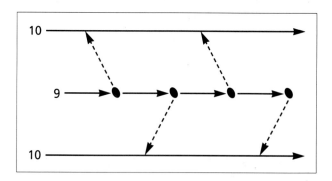

(i)   Pass inside to forwards – inter-passing before presenting rucked ball again.

(ii)   Pass outside to a three-quarter or forward who is standing off. He passes inside to the forwards.

(iii)   As above, but 9 receives an inside pass or loops to receive on the outside of the forward who was standing off.

🏉   Receivers A, B, C and D roll the ball back to the scrum-half. Coach calls what type of pass to make, and to whom.

🏉   The no. 8 acts as a flanker. The fly-half rolls the ball for him.

8 retrieves and gives to 9, who passes to 10. 10 rolls the ball again, etc.

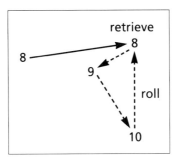

FLY-HALF ALIGNMENT

● Receiving a pass and selecting a line of run from a ruck or a maul. A, B, C and D are feeders. 10 receives the ball from alternate directions and passes to his centres. 10 is not always in the same position. Emphasise the importance of communication, calling 'Long!', 'Short!'.

Progression (i): add opposition flankers or a fly-half.

Progression (ii): have just one scrum-half to distribute each of the four balls.

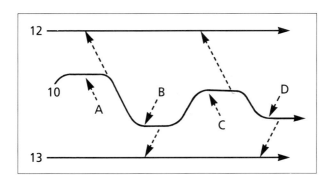

● Re-positioning on different balls. Slot into convenient places. Coach sets up delivery platform. (*See* diagram at top of next page.)

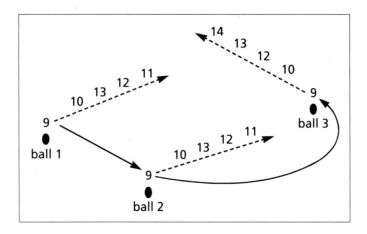

⬤ The scrum-half is on the 10-metre line with a supply of balls. The players are lined up on the other 10-metre line. The scrum-half has his back to them. He is fed the ball by a partner who collects them from the players on their way back.

(i) Each player in turn receives a pass from the scrum-half but shouts where he expects the ball, i.e. 'Short left/right!' or 'Long left/right!' The ball carrier runs on to the 22-metre line and jogs back. **Take a flat pass and cross the gain line quickly.**

(ii) As (i), but the players go in pairs. The second player must watch what the first is doing and try to get outside him to receive a pass. Tell the ball carrier where you are. **Both step into the pass and get on a straight running line.**

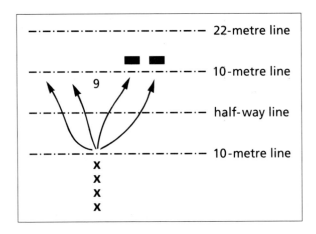

(iii) As (ii), but the receiver of the pass from the scrum-half must try to pass immediately, i.e. before the gain line. His support must cross the gain line at speed. **The first receiver may be under pressure if the back row is waiting.**

(iv) As (iii), but operate in threes. The first player passes to the second before the gain line, and the third player must tell the new ball carrier where he is supporting, i.e. on the inside or on the outside.

(v) As (iv). Now employ two defenders with tackle shields. First defender goes for the first ball carrier and the second defender goes for the second ball carrier, who puts the third attacker in the clear.

(vi) The scrum-half kicks either into the box or uses a grubber kick. The first player there either falls on the ball and pops it up to his two partners who inter-pass, or the first player goes beyond the ball, jumps, and collects and passes. He might tap the ball down, so the support must not go lateral but must come from deep.

(vii) The scrum-half is now paired up with a fly-half, who must do all the kicking (not too far). Three to chase the kick as (v).

● As the last exercise, but from line-outs. One throws to each of two jumpers in turn, who distribute to a scrum-half.

(i) The scrum-half passes flat and short to a forward when thrown to 2, and passes wide to the fly-half when thrown to 4.

(ii) Add extra players so that players go in twos and then threes.

(iii) The fly-half kicks for 2 or 4 to chase.

(iv) When thrown to 2, the scrum-half kicks for the forwards to chase.

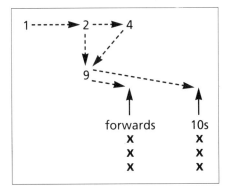

MIDFIELD RUNNING LINES

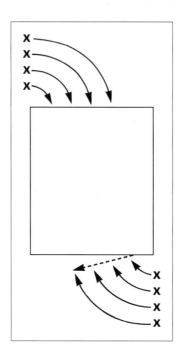

● (i)   Move in echelon, i.e. do not move until after the player immediately in front has moved. Run on an arc, i.e. turn into the pass to prevent outward drift. Get the ball to the wing before the grid line is crossed, and do not run into touch. Keep the space on the outside.

(ii)   Add a miss pass and an inside pass.

● As above, but a continuous stream. Jog the widths, and sprint around the corners and the lengths until the next line. Come back doing the same thing, avoiding the waves coming through.

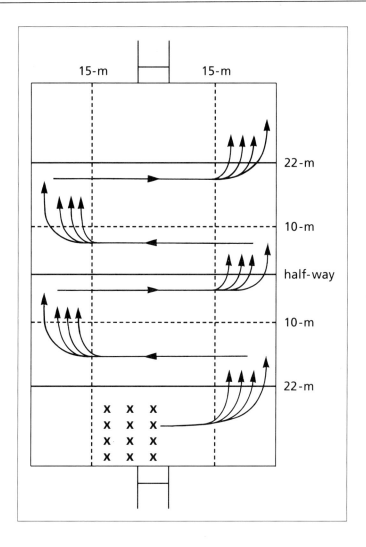

● The ball is moved to the wing before the gain line. Only the winger is allowed to touch the gain line with the ball in his hands. He puts the ball down on it. The scrum-half runs across to re-distribute the ball. Meanwhile, the three-quarters have followed the ball and run around it to come back in the opposite direction. Be aware of touch lines, and straighten up. This is first phase possession going into second phase.

Add an opponent from second phase who runs at the inside of each player. The players then have to step into the pass to 'fix' or 'draw' this cross cover before passing. Again, only the winger

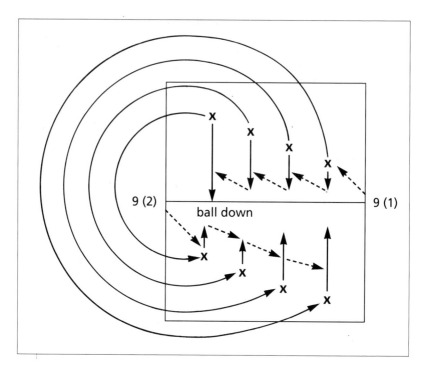

is allowed to get to the gain line with the ball, otherwise the second attack is not coming from depth. (*See* diagram above.)

● 3 v 3. Attackers run on an arc and aim for the defender's inside shoulder before making the pass. Do not pass too early or too late. (*See* diagram below.)

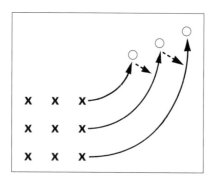

● Three lines of passive defenders (cones). 4 v 3. Attackers must get on to the correct running lines to create overlap and take out defenders. (*See* diagram at top of next page.)

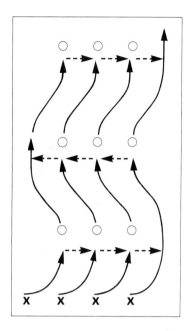

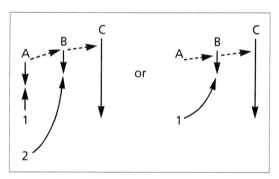

Jog through this exercise. A passes early. B draws the second defender and times his pass to put away the winger (C). The winger hangs back to accelerate on to the pass. B slows down if he is under pressure to get away the pass. (*See* diagram above.)

Go through, turn round, re-organise and come back.

Fix the defender by aiming for his inside shoulder. Pass before the contact to stay free to support.

Progression (i): defender 2 can go either for B or C. B must decide whether to pass or dummy. If the pressure is on the outside man, hold on to the ball. If it is on you, then pass.

Progression (ii): 2 now stands opposite B and further apart. A runs with the ball and passes late to put B under pressure. B must decide whether to pass or hold on, and wait for A to come in and help him.

Progression (iii): fours. A makes his pass to B, then runs behind the defender to become a second defender. (*See* diagram below.)

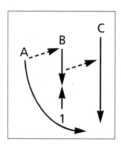

B could loop C, or C could draw A to the outside and pass inside to B.

EVASION

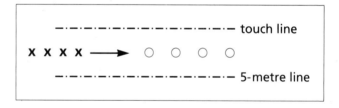

 (i)   Defenders (o) kneel and try to trip runners (x).
(ii) Defenders kneel but can fall sideways to trip each runner.
(iii) Defenders crouch but can fall sideways.
(iv) Defenders crouch but can dive and tackle.

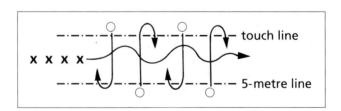

 os walk/jog constantly between the touch and 5-metre lines. xs run between, avoiding contact.

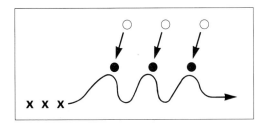

● x runs towards the cones, swerves away and then towards the next cone, and away again, etc. Each defender in turn runs towards the cone near him but not beyond it, so the attacker can get his lines of running correct.

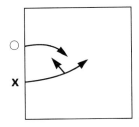

● (i) Attacker x gets five points if he comes inside the defender o with a side step. He gets one point if he goes outside the defender with a swerve.

(ii) Reverse the points to encourage the swerve.

(iii) Add a second attacker and defender. The first attacking player draws the first defender to release the second attacker to beat the second defender. (*See* diagram below.)

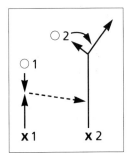

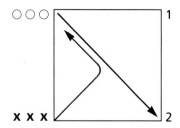

● The defender (o) jogs for corner 2 and keeps on running. The attacker (x) jogs for corner 1 but before colliding with o he drives off his outside foot, coming inside o to head for the defender's corner. (*See* diagram above.)

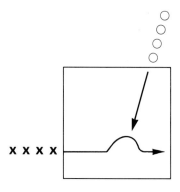

● The attacker (x) runs to score on the opposite grid line while the defender (o) tries to stop him either with a proper tackle or with a touch. Swerves should be employed to hold the defender before accelerating away again. (*See* diagram above.)

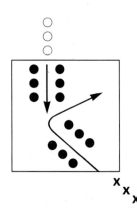

On the whistle, the attacker (x) runs through the tunnel made of cones and tries to score on the grid line on the right. At the same time the defender (o) runs through his own tunnel and tries to stop him. (*See* diagram at bottom of previous page.)

The coach stands in front of a queue of runners. As each comes out in turn to run at him, he raises either his left or right arm when they are a few metres away and the runner has to react by going to the opposite side of the coach to the raised arm.

Dummy

In fives or sixes; passing laterally.
(i) Jog together in a group. Keep passing. One player has to dummy and make a break; the rest have to react and support, and the movement starts again. Stay close
(ii) The receiver of the pass dummies to the person who passed to him, and then passes out.

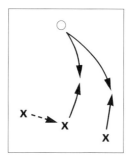

The first attacker just passes to the middle attacker, who has to cope with a 2 v 1 situation. The defender either goes for the ball carrier or for the outside man. The ball carrier must decide whether to pass or to hold on to the ball. (*See* diagram above.)

If the pressure is on the outside man, hold on to the ball. If the pressure is on the ball carrier, he should release the outside man.

Fend-off

In fours. One pair is in front with the ball, and the other pair is behind in support. Jogging pace. The first pair keeps passing the ball. On the whistle, whoever does not have the ball tries to tackle the ball carrier, who fends him off. The next pair takes over, either having to pick up the ball or receive a pass from the ball carrier. Continue the movement.

In pairs. One player holds the ball in one arm and leans against his partner as if fending him off. Change arms.

One partner in front support position, like an American football line-backer. His partner stands opposite about 2 metres away, and there is a ball on the ground between them. Pick up the ball and drive into the standing player.

In fives. One player faces the other four, who have been numbered off. The one player has a tackle shield and a ball. The coach shouts a number and the nominated player drives into the shield. The shield holder must retain possession of the ball.

Run the gauntlet. Players try to spill the ball out of the ball carrier's hands by slapping him. Fend off the slaps and dip the shoulder.

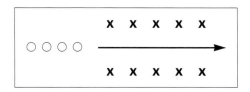

Defenders may start by holding out their inside arm so that the ball carrier drives through, brushing aside these arms and protecting the ball.

In threes. Player 1 tries to catch 2 while 3 fends off and carries a ball at the same time. No holding allowed.

The defenders kneel. The attackers weave in and out, handing off the defenders as they try to tackle. Transfer the ball to the outside arm. Defenders now crouch.

Variation of pace

In pairs, running in a straight line across the pitch.

(i) Run 15 metres at half-speed; increase this to just below top speed for 10 metres, and then accelerate to top speed for the next 10 metres.

(ii) Try variations in this order.

(iii) Both players stand 1 metre apart. The ball carrier must run in a straight line and can only use a variation of pace. The tackler must touch the ball carrier twice in quick succession as they run across. How many double touches can he make?

TACKLING

Front

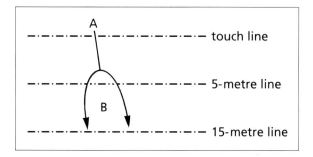

A to beat B to score on 15-metre line.

Attackers (x) to beat defenders (o) and re-join the line. If x is tackled successfully, he takes the place of the tackler and o gets up and tries to run through; if he is tackled he takes the place of the tackler. Runners should also be ball carriers.

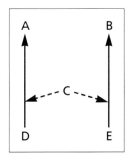

D and E run together. C feeds one of them the ball. He must try to beat the tackler in front of him.

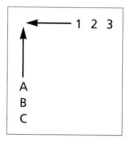

🏉 A and B pass. The player with the ball tries to beat the defender. After the tackle the support player picks up and tries to beat the second defender.

Side

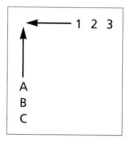

🏉 A, B and C run in turn and 1, 2 and 3 tackle in turn, then join the other line.

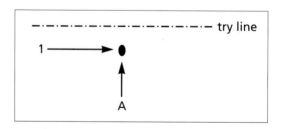

🏉 2 metres apart. A starts on his knees and has to pick up the ball and score. Tackler 1 moves as soon as A picks up the ball. Then A starts from the press-up position, and then from on his feet.

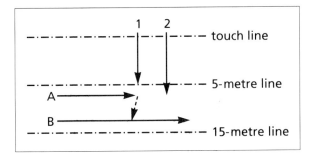

🏉 A draws 1 and passes to B, who must score by beating 2 on the outside.

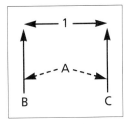

🏉 1 is the tackler. A is a feeder of the ball, with his back to 1. B and C run at the same time. A passes to one of them and 1 has to react quickly to tackle the ball carrier.

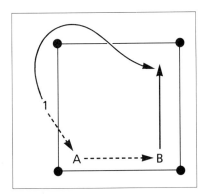

🏉 1 passes the ball to A, who passes to B immediately. B must score on the grid line. 1 must run around the grid cone and tackle B.

Rear

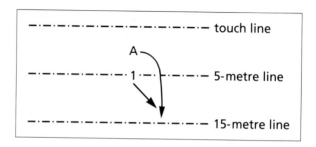

- (i) A and 1 face the 15-metre line. A stands 1 metre behind 1, who is on the 5-metre line. A chooses when to run past 1. 1 must tackle him before he scores on the 15-metre line.
- (ii) Start on the touch line with A in front of 1, and put the ball on the 5-metre line. A must pick up, and 1 can only tackle him when he has the ball in his hands.

1 trots with the ball and 2 tackles him from behind. 3 picks up and trots 5 metres before 4 tackles him. 5 picks up and 1 tackles him, etc.

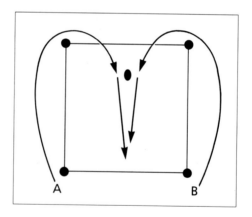

A and B run around the grid cones and race to pick up the ball to score on the grid line. The slower player must tackle the ball carrier before he scores.

In pairs with a ball. Start on the goal line, one behind the other. The ball carrier is the one at the rear. Both jog forwards, the ball carrier holding the ball against his partner's back. On the signal, the ball carrier has to get back to the goal line and his partner has to tackle him.

Exercises with tackle bags

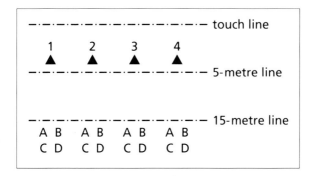

● Tackle bags are held up by players. Each bag is numbered. There is a ball on top of each bag.

(i) Partnered off, each player takes it in turn to tackle the bag, and the other retrieves the spilled ball. Secure the ball if it goes loose, i.e. go to ground if the ball is on the ground, and then quickly get up.

(ii) The tackler must now get to his feet quickly after the tackle to receive a pass from his partner.

(iii) Turn it into a race to score on a far grid line. The scorer returns the ball to the bag on the way back. Touch the next pair, who then go.

(iv) In threes. One tackles, the other two players run around the bag. The first one to the ball secures it and passes to the other player as they counter-attack towards their starting position.

(v) One player holds the tackle bag. The next runs to the touch line, turns and tackles the bag, then takes the holder's place. The third hits the bag from the front and takes the holder's place, and the sequence starts again.

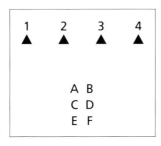

● (i) A number is called and the first pair races to tackle the nominated bag first.

(ii) If the player losing the race knows he is losing, he may tackle the winner before or as he tackles the bag.

(iii) While the players are running, the coach may nominate another bag so that they have to change direction.

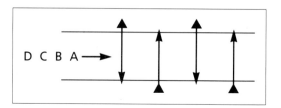

🏉   A, B, C and D tackle each bag in turn as they are dragged across from grid line to grid line and back again.

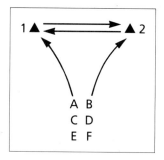

🏉   (i)   A goes for tackle bag 1 while B goes for 2. They quickly get up out of the tackle and tackle the other bag, then race back to re-join their line. Then the next pair goes. With small numbers, it could be a relay race.

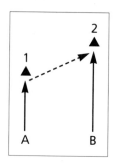

🏉   Tackle bag 1 has a ball on top. A and B start at the same time. A tackles 1 and then gets up quickly to secure the ball as B tackles 2 and the ball is spilled. B then gets up quickly to receive a pass from A.

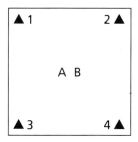

Four tackle bags are situated in the four corners of a grid. Two tacklers are in the middle of the grid. The coach nominates the tackle bag to be hit. The tacklers race to see which reacts the quicker. Shout another number as they are racing to the bag originally nominated. Make sure they do not hassle each other.

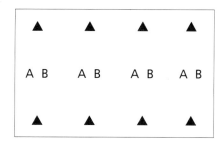

Each tackle bag is held and there is a ball on the top of each. There are two players in the middle. The As tackle both bags in turn. Each B has to pick up the spilled ball and hand it back to the bag holder. Make six tackles. Time it.

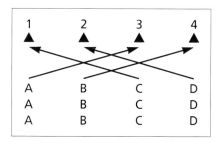

Tacklers A to tackle bag 3; tacklers B to tackle bag 4; tacklers C to tackle bag 1; tacklers D to tackle bag 2. Each tackler replaces the holder. Stage a relay race.

Tackling games

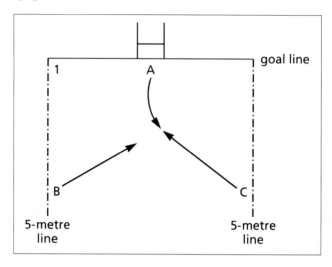

The first player from team C to score in corner 1. One player from team A and one from team B attempt to stop him. Which team scores the most tries?

6 v 6 in a grid. Coach gives the ball to a player who is not allowed to pass, or run across, or side-step. He must try to run straight and through the defenders' tackles. After each tackle the ball is returned to the coach.

Rugby league re-starts. Pass, and the receiver must run and attempt to score.

Team A on a grid line and team B a few metres away. Murder ball. How many of team A can get to the opposite grid line without being tackled?

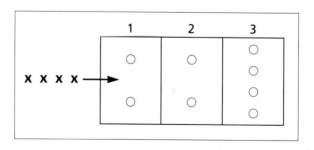

(i) Three grids. Eight defenders in total who stay in their own specified grid. One attacker at a time tries to score by running through each grid to the end. The tacklers try to stop him. The attacker gets a point for getting past the first grid, an extra point for getting past the next grid, and another for getting through the last one.

(ii) Release the attackers one after the other very quickly, so that the defence has little time to re-organise.

(iii) The attackers may go in pairs with a ball.

CONTACT AND BALL RETENTION

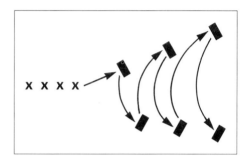

⬤ Each player carries a ball and hits each tackle shield in turn. The ball is carried in two hands and moved away from the shield.

Run with a low body position to create a wide and strong base when the contact is made. The last stride is a long one. Turn slightly so that contact is made with the hip.

Progression (i): the tackle shields advance to attack the ball carrier and give him less time to recover from the previous hit.

Progression (ii): the tackle shields catch the ball carrier off guard and cut down his recovery time. The ball carrier must get low and keep swivelling.

⬤ One ball carrier stands in the middle of a circle of five tackle shield holders. Hit a shield and then drive off to hit another. Remember the key factors. 30 seconds' work.

Progression (i): one ball between two. The ball carrier hits a shield. His support moves in and rips the ball away, and goes to hit another shield. The first ball carrier is now the support and moves in to take the ball. 30 seconds' work for each pair.

Progression (ii): the tackle shields provide sterner opposition and advance to catch the ball carrier off guard. Allow the two players some room and time.

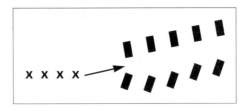

⬤ Tackle shield holders create a gauntlet. The ball carriers drive through the limited gaps. Leg power is important: keep pumping the legs. The shields may get progressively closer to provide tougher opposition.

⬤ A forward is paired off with a three-quarter. A ball is between them. On the signal, the forward tries to get the ball off the three-quarter, who resists as best he can without going to ground.
Progression (i): the same two files, with 2 metres between them, but the coach is in the middle with the only ball. The coach goes along the gap and gives the ball to either an x or an o. His partner then tries to get the ball off him. When the coach shouts 'Give!', the ball carrier returns the ball. Now the coach moves to another pair.
Progression (ii): the two files move closer and the tackler has to deck the ball carrier, who must present the ball properly. Then move even closer – eye to eye.

⬤ Auckland exercise in a grid with up to eight players in each corner. A ball is in each corner. Four tackle shield holders are in the middle of the grid, one facing each corner. Run across the grid in pairs.

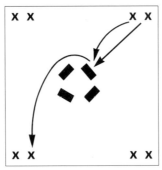

The ball carrier has to hit the shield; the support player moves in, rips the ball out and rolls off to make his way to his opposite corner, where he hands the ball on to the waiting pair. The ball may be passed also after the contact in the middle.

KICKING AND CATCHING

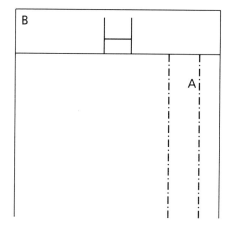

⚫ A stands either on the touch line, or on the 5-metre line, or on the 15-metre line. He is 5 metres from the goal line, and B is diagonally opposite.

A gets one point for **punting** the ball across the goal line to the near side of the posts; two points for the far side of the posts; three for through the posts. The same for **drop kicks** and **place kicks**.

⚫ A and B **punt** along the goal line at one post or over the posts. The same for **place kicks** and **drop kicks**.

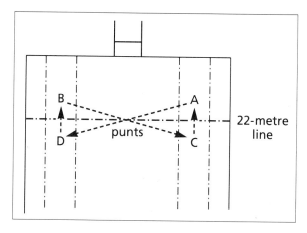

⚫ C passes to A, who **punts** to D. D passes to B, who kicks to C, etc. Keep changing the passers and kickers. The same for **drop kicks**.

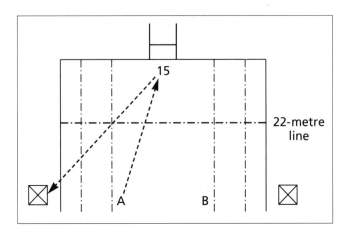

⬤ A and B have a supply of balls. They take it in turns to kick to the full-back. After fielding A's kick, the full-back **punts** to the nearest touch line, aiming at the target which is a grid just in touch. There may be a fielder in both grids to return the ball to A and B.

The full-back then touches the goal posts to show the next kicker that he is ready. B then kicks and the full-back fields and kicks the ball to the nearest touch line, again aiming at the grid.

A and B may **drop kick** to the full-back or try the **bomber kick**.

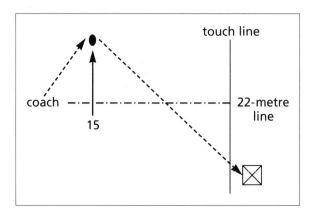

⬤ The coach places or rolls the ball behind the full-back into the 22-metre area. The full-back has to turn, collect the ball and find touch, aiming at the target grid.

Practise on both sides of the field. The full-back should be using his left foot to the left touch line because it is shielded from pressure by an opponent.

Practise different ways of collecting the ball, e.g. falling on it and getting up, fielding a rolling ball or one that is stationary, or one that is still in the air as he is running back so that he has to collect it over his shoulder.

Add a defender to exert some pressure on the fielder.

This exercise develops **punts** and **grubber kicks**.

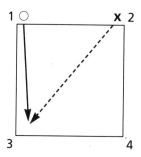

x kicks to corner 3 so that o has to run and catch it. o then kicks to corner 4 so that x has to run and catch it. x then kicks to corner 1 for o, and o kicks to corner 2.

The emphasis here is on accurate kicks and fielding while running to the ball, rather than catching when standing still.

Use the **punt** or **drop kick**.

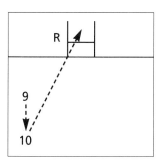

The scrum-half passes to the fly-half, who takes a **drop kick** at goal. The retriever (R) returns the ball to the scrum-half who now passes from a different field position.

Add a defending flanker to pressurise the kicker.

Kick-offs. A **drop kicks** for B, who jumps and taps the ball back for C.

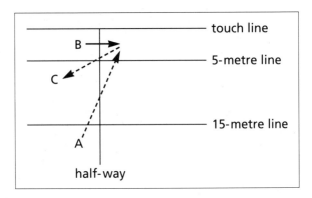

A may take the ball further into the middle, and also take **place kicks**.

🏉 In groups of five. One to kick each time. Moving up and down the field.

(i) Pass to the end of the line and the end player **cross kicks**. Gather the ball and repeat.

(ii) Two or three passes, and the ball carrier has to execute a **bomber kick**. All chase. One player leaps up and gathers the ball in, then distributes or taps it back. Another player should be a sweeper. More passing and repeat.

(iii) As (ii), but a **grubber kick**.

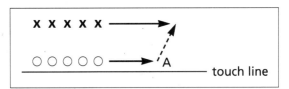

🏉 In pairs. *o* runs towards defender A and **cross kicks** to partner (x) running in the middle of the field.

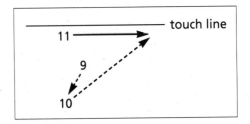

🏉 Similar to last exercise. The scrum-half (9) passes the ball to the fly-half (10), who kicks into the box for the winger (11) to chase and collect. **Bomber kick.**

Scrum-half box kick: face the touch line to protect the kicking leg; keep the eyes on the ball and the head down; hit the centre of the ball with the top of the foot; follow through with the kicking leg slightly across the body

● Stand behind the goal posts. Run and **chip** over the cross-bar, and catch the ball.

● Stand on the goal line. Make a **bomber kick** over the uprights and run to catch on the goal line on the other side of the posts.

● All stand on the goal line with a ball. All put up a **bomber kick** and chase and catch. Stage a competition to see how far players can get successfully.

● In fours. 1 and 2 on the goal line; 3 and 4 on the 22-metre line. In single files.

(i) 1 runs and **grub kicks**. He collects and hands on to 4, who does the same and hands on to 2, etc.

(ii) As (i) but one from each end run at the same time. Before they meet in the middle, the ball carrier **chip kicks** over the advancing player.

(iii) 1 **bomber kicks** and arrives to catch the ball. He hands on to 4, etc.

● A and B **grub kick** to each other. Each scores a goal if he gets it past his partner between touch and the 5-metre line, and across a grid line. Vary the distance between each kicker.

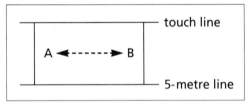

● In a grid. Either 2 v 2 or 2 v 1.

(i) **Chip kick** to partner. No charge downs: fairly passive opposition. Possession is lost if the ball is dropped or if it goes out.

(ii) **Grubber kicks.** Partner has to fall and gather in the ball, get up quickly and return the kick.

● **Scrum-half positional kicks.**

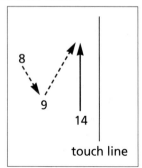

(i)   8 feeds the scrum-half, who **grubber kicks** for the winger to chase. Also use the kick to touch.

(ii) Now use the **bomber kick**.

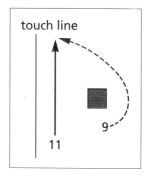

(iii) Other side of the field. The scrum-half kicks into the box over the heads of the scrummaging forwards.

🏉 **Fly-half positional kicks.**

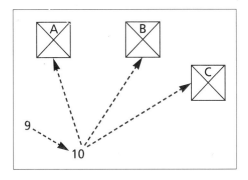

(i)   With a supply of balls, the scrum-half feeds the fly-half who kicks into the box (A) or towards the posts (B) or on the diagonal (C) to grid targets occupied by ball collectors.

(ii) Add an opposition flanker.

(iii) Add chasers.

(iv) Try from the other side of the field.

Kicking games

🏉 **Gaining distance game.** Use the whole pitch. Two sides with about ten players in each.

(i)· Kick the ball into space to drive the opposition back. If the opponent catches the ball cleanly, he may take ten strides forwards. Otherwise, he must kick from where he retrieves the ball.

If the ball is kicked into touch, he re-starts 15 metres in. If the ball is kicked over the dead ball line, the re-start is from the 22-metre line.

Three points are awarded for a successful conversion of a place kick; two for a drop kick; one for a punt.

(ii) As (i), but players may go anywhere and may kick to their own players. The opposition can intercept but not tackle. There are no charge downs of kicks.

(iii) Kick only with left foot. Only drop kicks, etc.

Kicking tennis. A kicks to B and B kicks back. The ball must land in the grid. There is an intervening out-of-court grid area. The ball must be kicked above shoulder height. If the ball is caught, no points are awarded.

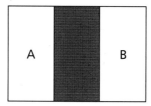

One point is awarded to the kicker if the ball is dropped, if the ball is caught but the catcher steps out of the grid, or if the ball lands in the defender's grid.

Have two in each grid. The catcher must pass to his partner, who takes the kick.

Play first to ten for each set, and the best of three sets.

COUNTER-ATTACKING

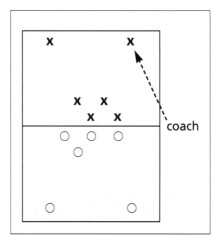

🏉 (i)   The coach kicks or throws the ball to each side in turn. That side then has to counter-attack. There are always two players deep on either side who take the counter-attack decisions. The one not catching should slot in behind the player who is, and take the decisions for him. Bring the ball forwards quickly. Support the ball carrier by getting back behind him.

(ii)   Overload the counter-attacking side by 4 v 2 or 5 v 3, so that the ball has to be moved quickly to exploit the numerical advantage.

🏉 (i)   In threes and in waves. The coach kicks to each wave in turn. One player acts as full-back, one is the open-side winger and the other is the blind-side winger. They counter-attack and work together in close support over a given distance.

(ii)   Add a defender, who starts alongside the kicker.

🏉 These drills involve scanning, decision-making and are relevant to the break-down of play in midfield, or the chip over the midfield and the quick counter-attack.

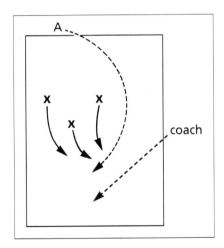

(i)   A throws the ball over the three counter-attackers (x), who retrieve the ball and score against A. The coach alternatively may roll the ball behind the three xs.

(ii)   The xs face A. The coach puts the ball down somewhere behind them. On the command 'Now!' they have to turn, assess and counter. Vary the numbers defending and attacking.

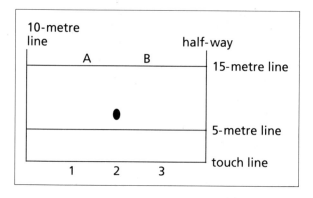

On the command 'Go!', everyone runs towards the ball. 1, 2 and 3 should arrive there first. They have to pick up and beat A and B to score on the 15-metre line.

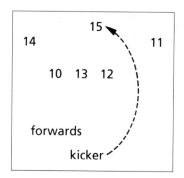

(i)   The ball is kicked out of defence. The three-quarters counter, opposed by either a set of three-quarters or a set of forwards.

(ii) Kick two, three or four balls in quick succession. Each ball should be retrieved and an attack launched. Then the next one can be kicked and the whistle blown so that the counter-attackers leave the previous ball and retrieve the next one.

(iii) Vary the numbers and the positions of the support and the opposition.

Use the width of the 22-metre area. 5 v 3. Three defenders (o) kick the ball out of defence. The five attackers (x) counter and score by working the ball to space and overlapping, rather than by individual evasion. (*See* diagram at top of next page.)

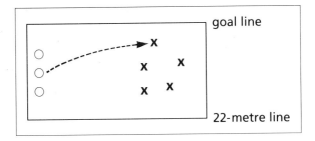

🏉 Two channels. Five defenders in one channel have to prevent five attackers from scoring in the same channel. They may use holding tackles. When the coach believes play has broken down or a try has been scored, he throws another ball into the other channel and shouts 'Counter!'. All players have to retreat to their own goal line and enter the second channel around a corner post. The first one to the ball claims it and his team have to score within the new channel.

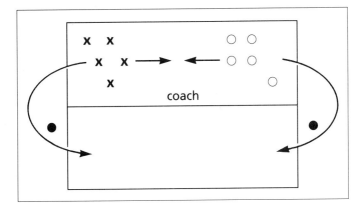

The coach may condition the game so that the original defenders get to the new ball first by rolling it nearer to their goal line.

Five players jog back towards their own goal line. Three or four defenders jog behind them, varying their formation. The player who originally passed the ball runs in front of his own line and decides where he wants to come into that line and receive a pass, so that he can bring the ball forwards towards the defenders. The rest of his line must then turn and support him.

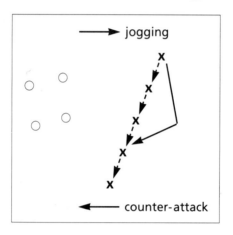

Rugby baseball. Two back lines. One team is fielding.

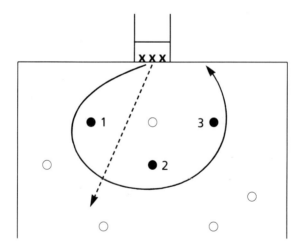

One team is under the posts. The players take it in turns to kick the ball out of defence. They are not allowed to kick the ball directly into touch. Other conditions may be imposed to make sure the fielding team do not find it too difficult.

Once the batting player has made his kick, he must run to cone 1 and pick up another ball. There should be a supply of balls here. He must run around cones 2 and 3 and race to score anywhere on the goal line.

The fielding team must collect the ball that was kicked. Everyone must handle the ball without forward passes. They must bring the ball forwards as quickly as possible to score also on the goal line. If they score first then the batting player is out. If the batting player scores first, then he has scored a run.

Each of the batting side must kick. They should use the ball that the previous runner has brought back and kick as soon as they are ready to ensure plenty of movement and little rest time.

PART III

UNIT EXERCISES

ALIGNMENT FROM SET PIECES

This is to be used as a basis from which to adapt the specific needs of a particular line. Basic principles must be stressed.

Work in the channel of the touch line to the 15-metre line and towards the half-way line. A scrum-half works with four players. He begins his pass from the half-way line, and the ball has to get to the winger before he crosses the half-way line.

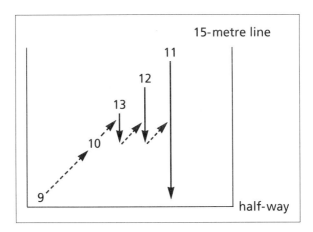

All players must run straight and fast. If these conditions are to be successful, then the players must not creep forwards. They should only move when the ball is in the inside player's hands. This includes the fly-half. When they move they must be accelerating on to the ball as fast as they can. Delay your run.

Progression (i): now add cones just in front of the half-way line to represent the tackle line. If players are to get their passes in before that line, they again will have to re-position themselves. So much will now depend on the ability of each individual to pass quickly and accurately under pressure.

Progression (ii): now add some opposition who may walk (then later jog) towards the attackers. Drop one opponent out so that it is 4 v 3, and there is always an overlap.

Progression (iii): to establish continuity and second phase ball, the winger places the ball on the half-way line and the whole three-quarter line runs around the ball to come down the same channel in the opposite direction. The scrum-half runs across to collect the ball and distributes it to the first player around. All players must handle the ball, **before** the half-way line is reached. Come from deep, run straight (not on an angle) and slot into the line wherever you can. It is difficult for the winger who placed the ball to get back out on to the wing again.

Race two or three lines against each other. Each line faces the half-way line. On the command 'Go!', the scrum-halves distribute to their respective lines. Only the winger from each line is allowed to cross the 10-metre line and it is a race to see who will score on half-way.

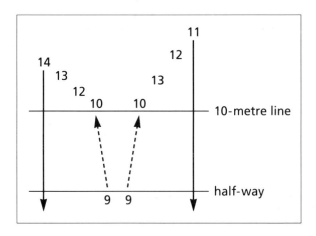

Progression (i): the ball always gets to the winger before the 10-metre line, but vary the player who has to score on half-way. The only players allowed to cross the 10-metre line are the winger and the nominated player, e.g:

– the fly-half has to receive an inside pass from the winger
– the outside centre must loop the winger to score
– use a full-back who enters the line between the outside centre and the winger. The winger scores from the full-back's pass.

Progression (ii): add a defender. A back row player could stand next to the scrum-half and oppose on a second command 'Go!'

RE-ALIGNMENT FROM BROKEN PLAY

Three three-quarter lines can be catered for on a rotational basis, i.e. two lines working and one resting. The lines can be any number from 5 to 7.

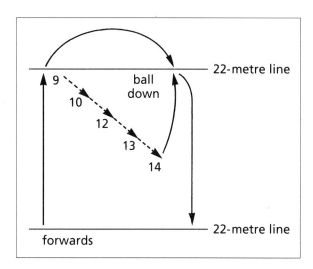

One unit acts as forwards and executes close passes from one 22-metre line to the other 22-metre line. Any lines can be chosen. When the players get to the far 22-metre line they put the ball down. The scrum-half passes it to the fly-half, and it goes along the line to the winger.

The winger must put the ball down on the 22-metre line. No three-quarter is allowed to cross the 22-metre line (the gain line) with the ball in his hands, except the winger.

In the meantime, the forwards have run along the 22-metre line towards the ball. They run in front of the three-quarters and across their line of vision, and if the three-quarters are lying deep enough, running fast and passing quickly, the two units should not bump into each other.

The forwards pick up the ball that the winger has left on the 22-metre line and they return to the other 22-metre line, interpassing. The ball is put down on the line and the three-quarters who have turned and re-aligned must get the ball to the winger before crossing the line. The winger puts the ball down, the forwards have run to it and now pick it up and go through the same sequence again.

The ball is passed in the same direction each length, and therefore to the same winger. To prevent this, the forwards may run on a diagonal on their return run.

Run twice through and then all change.

Progression (i): the forwards put the ball down on the half-way line and the scrum-half passes it to the blind-side winger or to the full-back going down the narrow side. The ball is then passed back to the forwards for them to place on the 22-metre line.

Progression (ii): the ball is put down after a certain number of passes, e.g. five, and then distributed to the three-quarters. Then reduce this number to four, three, two and one so that the three-quarters have less time in which to turn and re-align, so they may have to slot in wherever they can.

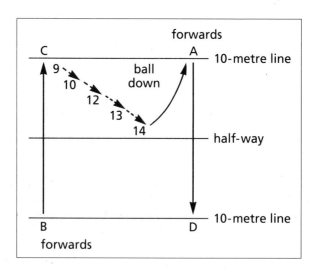

For two three-quarter lines. One three-quarter line is split up and acts as forwards operating between the two 10-metre lines. One group is on each line, on opposite sides, e.g. at A and B.

Those in group B run to the far 10-metre line, passing a ball. They put it down on the line and the scrum-half distributes to his three-quarter line. The three-quarters pass it to the winger, making sure they are running on to the passes and they do not cross the 10-metre line with the ball in their hands.

When the ball arrives at the winger, he puts it down on the line and the forwards of group A pick up and run to the opposite 10-metre line, passing the ball. They put it down and the three-quarters, who have turned and re-aligned, now get the ball and the winger puts it down on the line.

Rest, then give the ball to Group A at position D. They go again so that on both occasions this time the passing is off the right hand. Alternatively, a ball could be placed at positions C and D so that as soon as the winger has scored the forwards could pick up the new ball and go again, giving little rest to the three-quarter line, which has to turn and reform quickly.

● How to cope with 'pinched ball'. Two three-quarter lines, one acting as a group of forwards.

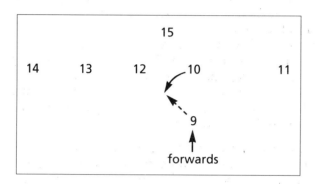

The forwards have the ball and inter-pass while jogging forwards. The three-quarters face them and back pedal.

On the command 'Now!', the forwards give the ball to the scrum-half who sets his three-quarter line in motion. The forwards have to stop them scoring.

The three-quarters should move the ball wide quickly with miss passes to get the ball away from the pressure areas. To get pace on the ball, the players lying deep should become involved.

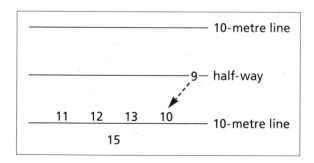

● The scrum-half stands on the half-way line with six balls. The ball is passed along the line to the winger who puts it down on the half-way line.

The three-quarters run on to the 10-metre line and turn. They re-align and return the other way.

This is done six times. The full-back enters the line on alternate runs.
Variation: one ball is used. The scrum-half runs across the half-way line to distribute the ball when it is put down by the winger. All passes go in the same direction.

A ball is placed on each of the 22-metre and 10-metre lines. The first ball is moved along the line to the winger before he crosses the line. Each player loops to receive another pass before he reaches the 10-metre line.

That ball is rolled away and the three-quarters re-align for the other ball on the 10-metre line. The same sequence happens: the ball goes to the winger before he crosses the line, then each player receives a pass by looping before the next 10-metre line.

That ball is rolled away and the three-quarters re-align on the next ball on the far 10-metre line.

A pattern of play. Unopposed, a three-quarter line moves the ball wide to the winger, who runs 5 metres and puts the ball down. The whole line re-aligns, going in the same direction, and moves the ball again. The ball is put down when it reaches the winger, and the three-quarters re-align to switch back in the other direction.

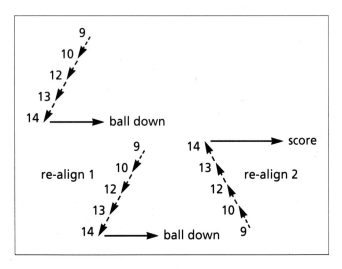

The full-back may come into the line on the first piece of action, and on the third. It is asking too much to expect him to join in on each movement.

Watch the gain and tackle lines. These may be marked out with cones.

Make sure the three-quarters are on straight running lines. Limit the width of the channel.

Progression: use the length of the pitch. Start with a scrum on the right. The scrum-half passes to the right winger, who runs 5 metres and puts the ball down. The three-quarters re-align and the ball is passed out to the left winger. He runs 5 metres and puts the ball down. The scrum-half now passes to the full-back, coming in down the narrow side.

The coach may blow his whistle to simulate tackles: the three-quarters have to re-align each time.

Opposition can be added, e.g. a fly-half and two centres, who must oppose only their opposite numbers. See if the attacking midfield can release its wingers.

The midfield may now drift on to the outside players so that the attacking midfield has to cope with more decisions.

● Two three-quarter lines, in opposition, spread out anywhere in the 22-metre area. The coach rolls a ball into the area and shouts 'Play!'. The team securing the ball first will be the attackers. The first player will be the scrum-half, and the rest re-align on him. After a count of five, the ball is released for the attacking side to score.

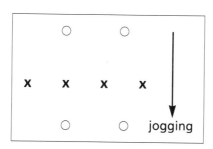

● The xs are in possession of the ball. There are two defenders in front and two behind. All of the players jog in the same direction and the ball is passed constantly. On the whistle, the attackers attempt to score and the defenders try to prevent them. If the defence succeeds in tackling the ball carrier, it sets up a counter-attack.

● A three-quarter line attacks the goal line from the 22-metre line. On the whistle, the ball carrier has to put the ball down. The nearest player acts as a scrum-half and the rest re-align. The ball is played after a count of three. Do not be lazy and do not

get flat. See the number of the player on the inside. Get behind the ball carrier and do not run in front. Call for the ball. Go in the same direction twice, and re-align to come back the other way.
Progression (i): build in a switch, or a loop, or a cut-out pass.
Progression (ii): the ball carrier decides and calls out what he wants to happen, e.g. 'Switch!' or 'Come in and get the ball!', or 'Loop!', etc.

REACTION TO THE BREAK

🏉 The three-quarters are grouped together and numbered off. 1 starts jogging in any direction, carrying a ball. He can choose any moment to sprint off for 10 metres, trying to lose the group. He shouts the number of one of the other players in the group, and then slows down. The nominated player must come and take a pass. Then he slows down, the group gets back together, and the sequence begins again.
Progression: the ball carrier may call two or three numbers. The first nominated player receives a pass and must pass to the second nominated player: if a third player has been called, he receives the next pass.

🏉 Two or three three-quarter lines are organised in waves on the half-way line. The first line is given the ball and a passing movement begins. On the command 'Break!', the ball carrier has to side-step and run 10 metres. He then puts the ball down. There must be immediate support to pick it up and continue the movement.
Progression (i): the first support player is told to pop the ball up immediately to a second support player coming close.
Progression (ii): when the first line has finished and reached the goal line, it turns and jogs back, getting in the way of the next line. The next line now has to take decisions, and one player will have to weave his way through before putting down the ball.
Support must be immediate. Support must come close and from depth.

🏉 As for the second drill in this section. After the 'break', the coach shouts for support on the inside or on the outside. The ball carrier must slow and pass to the nominated area: there should be support players present.
Progression: as for *progression (ii)* of the second drill.
Support should be on both sides of the ball carrier.

🏉 As above. After the 'break', the coach shouts 'Tackled!', and the ball carrier must stop and stand still on his feet. The nearest three-quarter, probably the player who has just passed to him, must go in, take the ball and continue the movement.

Progression (i): all players on the inside of the tackled player must be looping outside, and the player who first goes in to rip the ball must pop it up to one of these players.

Progression (ii): as above, but the coach shouts out a number. The first support player who has ripped the ball away must distribute to the nominated player. If '1!' is shouted, he must give to the first support player, and to the second if '2!' has been shouted.

Pass and support. Go through the same hole as that created by the breaking player. If the ball carrier is tackled, the player who passed to him is responsible for going in to secure the ball, and keeping the movement going if possible.

● Two lines, in opposition, practise the above exercises and principles.

Progression (i): nominate a player to attempt to make a break. If he is tackled, he must try to stay on his feet and wait until support arrives.

Progression (ii): an extra man comes into the line.

DECISION-MAKING

● In a channel. Two groups, four to six in each.

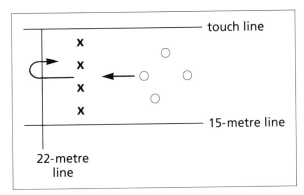

The attackers (x), with a ball, jog towards a designated line, e.g. the 22-metre line. They keep passing the ball. The defenders (o) jog behind them at the same speed and in a broken defence which will vary each time this drill is used.

When the attackers get to the 22-metre line, they turn and attack the defenders. The player with the ball must assess the situation when he turns, and take decisions about the direction in which to pass, or whether to run, etc.

Progression: let the defenders jog forwards with the attackers following them. Vary the starting positions of the defenders. The attackers keep passing the ball but they now have a better idea of where they will attack when the whistle goes for the defenders to turn and defend. The attackers will also be given some extra time as the defenders assess what they should be doing.

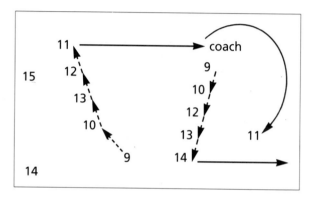

Starting from a set piece, the three-quarter line gets the ball to the winger. The full-back may come into the line. The winger runs forwards to the coach and delivers him the ball. The three-quarters re-align, attacking the same goal line, but either switching back or continuing to run to the open side. The winger now runs around the coach and tries to stop the line scoring.

Vary the defender so that everyone must slot into the line wherever they can, as if one of their line has been tackled and taken out of the game.

Nominate two defenders to run around the coach after they have passed. The attack must hold these defenders, who are running at them from angles.

Solutions: give long cut-out passes to get the ball to the fast wingers with plenty of space in which to move; run straight to fix the defenders and prevent them moving on to the outside players; dummy switch to make the defence think that the ball is coming back; pass inside and then out again.

Two channels, with three defenders in one and two in the other. At the head of the channel with two defenders there should be two attackers; at the head of the channel with three defenders there should be three attackers.

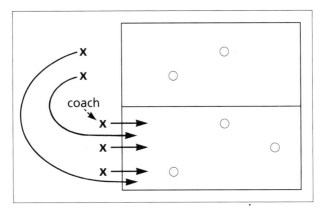

If the coach gives the ball to the two attackers, they must try to score without going outside their channel. The other three attackers must run around the coach to attack the same channel, and not go outside it. These attackers may be the back row taking the ball on after the break down. In the meantime, the remaining three defenders must stay out of it all.

If the coach gives the ball to the three attackers, *their* channel must be used, and they will be supported by the other two coming from deep. The two defenders stay out of it.

Three channels. One group of five with a ball, and another group of five to defend.

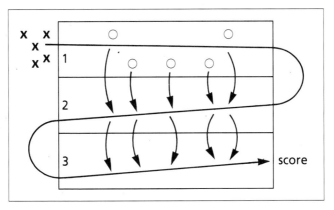

The attackers have to get to the end of channel 1, and immediately sweep around to get to the end of channel 2. Once they get to the end of this channel, they sweep around to score at the end of channel 3.

The defenders must not interfere with the ball. They must not interfere with the attackers when they get to the end of each channel. They can tackle properly or use holding tackles, or the drill can be conditioned to include touch tackling, so the ball carrier must pass immediately.

Once the defenders are beaten in channel 1, they move across to channel 2, and ultimately to channel 3. The defensive formation is thus constantly changing, and the attackers have to make many different decisions regarding space and numbers.

🏉 Two teams of five opposed to each other. One channel.

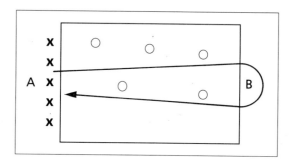

The attackers have to get to the end of the channel (position B), and immediately turn around to bring the ball back to position A, where they finally score.

The attackers have to take decisions because some of their number may be late arriving from the first attack: they may have been taken out by a tackle. The defence will also be re-grouping after the initial attack.

🏉 Two three-quarter lines in opposition. The coach manufactures a gap in the defence so that the ball carrier must take instant decisions as to whether to go through the gap himself or put someone else through it with a pass.

The coach may tell one of the defenders quietly that when the ball is in play, he must turn around and run backwards, or go up to defend slowly, or run up very fast and ahead of the other defenders.

The coach may give each of the defenders a number. When the ball comes in to play, the coach can call out a number and the nominated player should run backwards.

If the coach has called out '12!', the centre turns around and run backwards. 13 spots the gap and heads for it. The rest of the line must surge through to link up with him.

🏉 Two three-quarter lines in opposition in a limited space, say across the pitch, inside a 22-metre zone. Condition the defence.

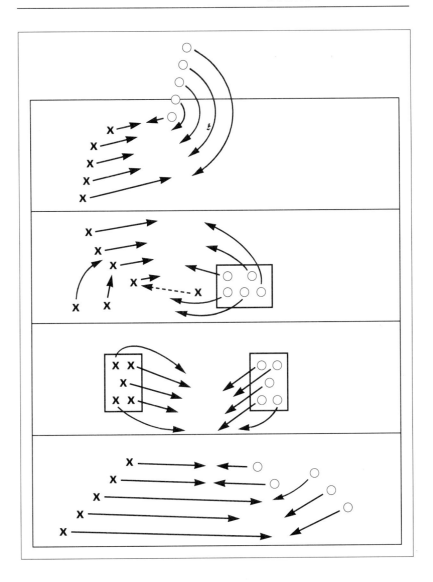

Play touch rugby, where the ball carrier must make a pass immediately he is touched. The defence may be allowed to tackle, but
must not interfere with the ball.

Condition the defence in some of the following ways:
- get them to lie down and offer resistance on the whistle
- get them to turn their backs on the attackers, then oppose on
  the whistle
- bunch them up as if they were forwards in a scrum

– organise them into a line-out formation
– break them up into two (or smaller groups), with different starting shapes, or starting to defend at different times
– decide where you are to arrange the space into which the
  attackers should be moving.

⬤ Two three-quarter lines playing in a restricted area. The
coach wanders about with a ball. The scrum-halves must stay
with him, and the other players continually re-position themselves on the ball. The coach then releases the ball to one of the
scrum-halves, and *his* three-quarter line tries to score.

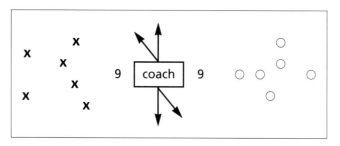

If there is a break down in play, the coach may introduce
another ball.

The coach may manufacture rucks by acting as a pack of forwards and releasing the ball on the ground while he is going forwards fast, and the opposition is back pedalling to stay onside.

The coach may simulate a maul going either forwards or backwards. If it is going backwards, the three-quarters will be under
pressure because they are back pedalling while the defenders are
coming forwards.

The coach can simulate a back peel from a line-out or a back-
row move, and then release the ball.

⬤ Two units. Simulated first phase possession. On the first
tackle, the team on the attack all move to that spot. As soon as
they arrive, the ball is given to the other team, who try to score.

The coach may give the second strike to the team first in possession. The defending team would then all move to the spot
where the first tackle was made, and the coach would release the
ball to the attackers again.

INDEX